INTRODUCTION
What Is Brand Storytelling?

We all have dreams. Paul's dream was to hike the 2,189-mile Appalachian Trail.

Paul Evans passed away before he could make his dream a reality. But, as it turns out, it wasn't the end of his story. It was the beginning. Thanks to the outdoor recreation company Recreational Equipment, Inc. (REI).

It started with an e-mail Paul's wife, M'Lynn, sent to *The Dirtbag Diaries* podcast. In it she talked about her husband of 17 years, about his kindness and self-lessness and the fact that all his life he was drawn to

America's most iconic trail. But Paul had a bad heart. He passed away two weeks shy of his fifty-fourth birthday, never setting foot on the trail. Months prior, Paul had taken great joy in preparing for that one last hike he so coveted, polishing his size-13 hiking boots.

M'Lynn wondered how great it would be for his boots to make that journey. In 2016 the podcast broadcasted her request, and 400 people answered the call. REI stepped in to help make Paul's dream a reality. And #PaulWalksOn was born.

REI didn't just launch a campaign, it sparked a movement. Paul's Boots brought together very different people with one goal: to take Paul on that hike.

2,189 miles.

40 hikers.

One man's dream.

The hikers carried Paul's Boots the entire length of the Appalachian Trail. Together, they wrote a different conclusion to Paul's story. And in the process, they formed new friendships, reached new heights, and discovered themselves. Explore their stories here: https://www.rei.com/blog/paulsboots.

REI is one of our all-time favorite brands. And not because its products are amazing (which they are), but because everything the company does, big or small, tells its story. It is a story of authenticity and caring.

It is an inspirational push to get every single one of us outdoors to experience nature and to find out what we are capable of. From major moves like shutting down its stores on Black Friday to encourage its employees and customers to #OptOutside to sending personalized tweets that make people feel heard, REI is the epitome of a brand that walks the talk and lives its mission.

"Where has this book been? The *Laws of Brand Storytelling* is a brilliantly crafted, approachable, and empowering resource for any business leader who wants their brand to stand out, engage customers, build loyalty, and garner more referrals. Rich with marketing wisdom, inspiring examples, and practical tools, *The Laws of Brand Storytelling* will help you effectively communicate your macro and micro brand stories in ways that engage and inspire. A must-read for anyone who wants to emotionally connect with and be remembered by prospects and customers alike."

—JOSEPH MICHELLI, #1 *New York Times* bestselling author
of *The Starbucks Experience, The New Gold Standard,*
The Zappos Experience, and *Driven to Delight*

"A solid guide filled with real-world examples of big brands making big moves. Exceptionally useful."

—JOHN GARGIULO, Global Product Marketing Lead, Airbnb

"This is—hands down—the best book ever written about brand storytelling! It is a page-turner jammed with compelling stories about telling stories. I couldn't put it down."

—JASON JENNINGS, *New York Times, Wall Street Journal,*
and *USA Today* bestselling author of *Less Is More,*
Think Big, Act Small, and *The Reinventors*

"A brand is nothing but a promise delivered. Making an emotional connection with your customers is what'll determine the success of your business. *The Laws of Brand Storytelling* is a comprehensive step-by-step guide to doing just that. Highly recommended."

—JEFFREY HAYZLETT, Chairman, C-Suite Network,
and bestselling coauthor of *The Mirror Test,*
Running the Gauntlet, and *Think Big, Act Bigger*

"In the era where your brand is shaped by customer experiences, Ekaterina and Jessica teach you how to define and deliver those experiences through the incredible, human power of stories."

> —BRIAN SOLIS, bestselling author of *X: The Experience When Business Meets Design*

"This terrific new book isn't just a strategic guide to brand storytelling. It also serves up a ton of inspiration!"

> —ANN HANDLEY, CCO, MarketingProfs, and *Wall Street Journal* bestselling author of *Everybody Writes*

"Ekaterina and Jessica capture the art and science of brand storytelling perfectly. The laws presented in their book should be every marketer's laws, no questions asked. Every storyteller should heed the advice they provide, regardless of where they are in their career. It'll not just make for better marketing, but better business."

> —SHIV SINGH, former SVP of Marketing, Visa Inc., and author of *Savvy*

"The power of brands lies in the stories that they tell. Advertising is only a small (and getting smaller) part of the story. In *The Laws of Brand Storytelling*, Ekaterina and Jessica really dig deep to help you (and your business) figure out how to win in a world where price and distribution is a losing position to bank on. Brands matter more than ever. Tell a better brand story, build a business forever—that's what it's all about."

> —MITCH JOEL, author of *Six Pixels of Separation* and *Ctrl Alt Delete*

"Every time you buy a brand, what you're really buying is a story. It's a story you hear in your head and feel in your heart. This amazing compendium of brand storytelling's unwritten rules shows you exactly where that story came from, and gives step-by-step instructions to start writing your own. If you own a brand, you need to know these rules."

> —DAN ROAM, bestselling author of *The Back of the Napkin* and *Draw to Win*

"*The Laws of Brand Storytelling* provides a solid framework and easy steps to humanizing your brand. A hugely valuable resource for individuals, brands, and startups alike!"

> —PAM DIDNER, author of *Global Content Marketing* and *Effective Sales Enablement*

THE LAWS OF
BRAND
Storytelling

WIN—AND KEEP—
YOUR CUSTOMERS'
Hearts
+ Minds

EKATERINA WALTER + JESSICA GIOGLIO

Mc
Graw
Hill
Education

New York   Chicago   San Francisco   Athens   London   Madrid
Mexico City   Milan   New Delhi   Singapore   Sydney   Toronto

1 2 3 4 5 6 7 8 9   LCR   23 22 21 20 19 18

ISBN   978-1-260-44019-5
MHID   1-260-44019-2

e-ISBN   978-1-260-44020-1
e-MHID   1-260-44020-6

Library of Congress Cataloging-in-Publication Data

Names: Walter, Ekaterina, author. | Gioglio, Jessica, author.
Title: The laws of brand storytelling : win -- and keep -- your customers' hearts and minds / by Ekaterina Walter and Jessica Gioglio.
Description: 1 Edition. | New York : McGraw-Hill Education, 2018.
Identifiers: LCCN 2018030682| ISBN 9781260440195 (hardback) | ISBN 1260440192
Subjects: LCSH: Marketing. | Storytelling--Economic aspects. | BISAC: BUSINESS & ECONOMICS / Marketing / General.
Classification: LCC HF5415 .W285 2018 | DDC 658.8/27--dc23 LC record available at https://lccn.loc.gov/2018030682

McGraw-Hill Education products are available at special quantity discounts to use as premiums and sales promotions or for use in corporate training programs. To contact a representative, please visit the Contact Us pages at www.mhprofessional.com.

CONTENTS

Introduction: What Is Brand Storytelling?. 1

CHAPTER 1 THE PROTAGONIST LAWS. 11
Know Who You Are

The Purpose Law. 14
The Visual Identity Law. 24
The Differentiation Law 29
The Authenticity Law 38
The Conflict Law 45

CHAPTER 2 THE STRATEGY LAWS. 59
Understand Your Goals

The Strategic Blueprint Law 60
The Collaboration Law 90

CHAPTER 3 THE DISCOVERY LAWS 93
Find Your Story

The Hero Law 95
The Actionable Intelligence Law 106
The Beyond-the-Obvious Law. 114
The Storyteller Law 120
The Law of Opportunity 124

CHAPTER 4 **THE STORY-MAKING LAWS** 131
Craft Your Story

The Consistency Law 132

The Simplicity Law 136

The Language Law. 138

The Visual Storytelling Law 148

The Diversification Law 156

The Quality Law. 171

The Humor Law 174

The Urgency Law. 177

The Utility Law 186

The Ownership Law. 191

The Brand Protection Law 193

The Optimization Law. 199

CHAPTER 5 **THE CHANNEL LAWS** 205
Share Your Story

The Personalization Law. 207

The Channel Mix Law. 211

CHAPTER 6 **THE LAWS OF ENGAGEMENT** 233
Engage with Your Communities

The Response Law 234

The Surprise and Delight Law 240

The Law of Humanizing Your Brand. 248

CHAPTER 7 **OH, ONE MORE LAW . . .** 253
Make Your Own

CONCLUSION 257

Acknowledgments 260

Notes 261

Index 270

Because here's the truth about branding. Branding isn't about your logo, the approved color palette, and cool taglines. Branding is about the stories that your communities create around your mission. Branding is about extraordinary customer service. Branding is about experiences every single person has with your company. And by "every single person," we mean anyone interacting with your brand: not just your customers but prospects, partners, investors, and employees as well.

A brand is the sum of interactions

(real and perceived) that a person has

with a company across all touchpoints.

In the age of the empowered consumer, your brand is not what you say it is. It is what they say it is.

Your brand identity isn't fixed. It's fluid. If you stay true to who you are and your mission in everything you do, you have a chance to build on it consistently with your everyday stories and strengthen your brand in the process.

Brand storytelling is at the core of your brand. It is a way of connecting with communities that share your values and your beliefs. Brand storytelling invites others into your tribe and embraces them in an authentic way. Brand storytelling equals heart marketing!

Brand storytelling isn't about creating

marketing campaigns, but building

tribes and inspiring movements.

Or, if you are looking for a more formal definition:

∽∾

**Brand storytelling is the art of shaping
a company's identity through the use of
narratives and storytelling techniques
that facilitate an emotional response and
establish meaningful connections.**

∽∾

Brand storytelling done right is never self-absorbed; it is a dialog. It's human and real and relatable. It doesn't have to be dramatic or even funny, but it unites, sparks conversations, and puts people first.

Storytelling can take the form of a video, a tweet, a conversation, a surprise-and-delight act, great customer service, or a brand taking a stand on a specific issue. The list is long. A company's *every* interaction with the world matters in shaping its story (both at the macro and micro level).

Macro stories are at the core of your organization's DNA. They highlight your company's story, its founding myth. They can do so through a logo, a brand identity guide, and the story of the founder(s). What drove the founder(s) to risk everything and start an enterprise? Why was it important? What challenges had to be overcome? How was the ultimate mission statement shaped? It is usually a story of human struggle and human triumph. Macro stories are the why, the foundation of and the reason for everything the company does.

Companies' macro stories are extremely powerful. Consider how Kraft Foods managed its 2010 integration of the British confectioner Cadbury. There was strong internal resistance to the acquisition within Cadbury. Its 45,000 employees openly expressed their concern for the loss of their values and decline in the quality of their product as a result of the move. The clash of cultures led many to believe that the acquisition would be a major disaster. But Kraft's senior executives turned to both companies' histories and DNA as a way to smooth the transition. They found evidence of shared values and similarities in their journeys. For example, both founders were deeply religious men, committed to their employees and the quality of their product. Both believed in giving back to their communities. The company created a site that offered interactive timelines, iconic images, historic video, and an illustration titled "Growing Together" that traced Kraft's previous mergers. All of it strongly showcased the similarities of the two cultures and expressed the desire to move forward as a united company. The result? One of the smoothest mergers in Kraft's history.[1]

Regardless of where or how we use our macro stories, they give us a strong sense of identity and purpose. They serve as the North Star in everything we do—from marketing, to sales, to customer service, and beyond.

Micro stories are the lifeblood of your storytelling strategy. They are an "always-on" approach to continue building on your macro story. They are the moments in time that allow us to keep our brand at the forefront of everyone's mind in a relevant way.

Micro stories can come in any shape or form: website updates, social content, blog posts, press releases, comarketing and partner messaging, packaging, events, customer stories, employee stories, influencer stories, internal communications, newsletters, e-mail campaigns, product delivery, and so on. The list is long.

What is critical to remember, however, is that there is an underlying consistency to those stories across channels, formats, and times. Your micro stories cannot contradict your macro story. They are designed to support and extend it.

Let's go back to our REI example. REI as a brand is extremely consistent about who it is and what it represents. Every single campaign, every single tweet, every single act by the brand supports its mission of "inspiring, educating, and outfitting its members and the community for a lifetime of outdoor adventure and stewardship."

The Paul's Boots campaign is just one example. Closing its stores on Black Friday for three years in a row is another.

Instead of promoting Black Friday shopping, in 2015 REI took a bold approach by proactively encouraging its employees and customers to #OptOutside. To do so, the company announced that it would close all of its retail locations and pay its employees as though it was a regular workday. The company said that its brand purpose was to get people outside, and it wanted to partner with its customers on Black Friday to get them to do something unprecedented. The brand shut down completely; it didn't even process online orders that day.

The #OptOutside campaign is hosted on a dedicated microsite where REI shares its goal for the campaign, highlighting: "Time outdoors makes you healthier and happier. And there are so many ways to get out. No need to be extreme. Just find a place near you, then open the door and head outside. Want to advance your

skills? There's an REI class for that (https://www.rei
.com/opt-outside)."

The microsite listed a range of activities that you
could do outdoors on Black Friday, such as camping,
hiking, climbing, and more. In addition, by putting
in your hometown, you could uncover local outdoor
activities to try. For example, by entering a Boston,
Massachusetts, zip code, we uncovered a recommendation for a tree run in Blue Hill South, a relatively
easy mountain biking ride to do with children, and a
trail hike featuring spectacular views of Boston.

To continue the conversation, the company shared
the images and stories of customers and employees who decided to #OptOutside on its social media
channels during the Thanksgiving and Black Friday
weekend, putting a human face on the movement.

The first year's campaign results were impressive,
with a 7,000 percent increase in social media mentions. The company's news also generated 2.7 billion
PR impressions in just 24 hours. In total, the campaign
generated 6.4 billion media impressions and 1.2 billion
social media impressions while inspiring 1.4 million
people to spend their day outdoors.[2]

Even better, other retailers decided to join REI in
closing their doors on Black Friday. In total, 150 retailers participated and hundreds of America's state parks
decided to open their doors for free to support the
#OptOutside movement.

What an impact! Talk about heart marketing!

REI's stories don't end there.

There was the time REI appeared in the Hollywood
movie *Wild* because of its amazing customer care. The
film is based on the memoir of the same title by Cheryl
Strayed, who midway through her 1,100-mile hike of

the Pacific Crest Trail lost her boots. She was able to call the company and it shipped her a new pair, no questions asked. That experience really stuck with Strayed, and made it into both the book and the movie. There was no product placement deal, mind you. Can this get any cooler?

Yes, it can. I (Ekaterina) had my own "wow" experience with REI. One eventful Christmas holiday, I tweeted at the company, asking, "What is the best gift suggestion you have this year?" Within 30 minutes I received a reply that included a custom video personally addressed to me and tailored to my interests. I promptly bought what REI suggested! I've included this example in our book *The Power of Visual Storytelling*, and I have since used it in several dozen of my keynotes. Talk about the power of word of mouth!

The world we live in is rapidly changing. Customer expectations are shifting, and customers' attention span is shrinking. Great marketing isn't just about grabbing attention with catchy taglines and clickbait headlines anymore, but holding that attention and building lasting and meaningful connections. Brands can no longer rely on slogans and jingles but must learn to tell stories.

Brand storytelling, however, will only be impactful if it is done holistically. From marketing campaigns, to everyday engagements with your customers on social networks, to your customer service, every act, every piece of content, every engagement tells a story. And every story adds to a person's perception of your brand.

In our previous book *The Power of Visual Storytelling: How to Use Visuals, Videos, and Social Media to Market Your Brand* we talk about the origins and importance of storytelling, as well as the rise and impact of social networks, and provide guidance on how to craft stories using rich media.

This book expands on that. It serves as a strategic guide to brand storytelling as a whole. It shows you how storytelling touches every aspect and function of your company. It walks you through what we call The Storyteller Journey (Figure I.1) and provides you with the blueprint for each step.

FIGURE I.1   The Storyteller Journey

Packed with strategic frameworks, inspiring stories and approaches, and helpful tips, *The Laws of Brand Storytelling* explores everything you need to consider in crafting your company's narrative, from where to source the best stories to how to present them.

Are you ready to dive in? Let's go!

Chapter 1

THE PROTAGONIST LAWS

KNOW WHO YOU ARE

In 2012, Rikke Rosenlund volunteered to take care of her neighbor's dog, Aston. Instead of being stuck indoors all day, Rikke and Aston, whom she describes as a "cute brown Labrador," spent an incredible afternoon together. They played in the park, attended a garden party, and even made some new friends.

The day sparked an aha moment for Rikke. It started as a favor to her neighbors: they trusted her and felt at ease leaving Aston with her for the day. However, after spending the afternoon with the Lab, Rikke realized that she was also getting something amazing in return: the joy of spending the day playing with an adorable dog.

In her own words: "I remember thinking, why are people spending so much money on dog walkers or kennels, or leaving their dog home alone, when I would love to take care of a dog for free? I thought, there should be a website where local dog owners could meet local people like me. This would benefit everyone. Dogs would get more love and attention. Owners would get some help from other dog lovers when they couldn't be with their own dogs, and then us borrowers would get the happy dog time."[1]

Inspired to help connect dog owners and dog lovers, Rikke founded Borrow My Doggy that same year. Fast-forward to 2017 and over half a million people in the United Kingdom and Ireland have signed up to use the site. The site operates on a membership model, where dog owners pay around £4 a month and dog borrowers pay just over £1 a month. Once signed up, the matching process is executed by an algorithm that suggests potential owners and borrowers based on location, availability, and the type of dog.

The company's purpose and mission is to "share the love of dogs." While Rikke knew that people would join because of their love of dogs, what she didn't realize is how Borrow My Doggy would help people in unexpected ways.

For example, there was a man who'd recently had an operation and needed help walking his dog during his recovery, an exchange student who deeply missed her dogs at home and found that borrowing other people's dogs brought her happiness, and a family with a little girl who was scared of dogs whom they wanted to introduce slowly to canine friends to see if she could overcome her fear.

Rikke realized that her mission to found the company was personal, and so were the stories of her members. Borrow My Doggy was doing more than just solving a problem—it was helping people with different needs based on a common passion: a shared love of dogs.

We didn't name this chapter "The Protagonist Laws" for companies to default to their brand as the hero of its story. With Borrow My Doggy, there are many heroes within its brand story, from an inspiring founder to all the dog owners and borrowers. Each hero takes center stage at different times over the course of the brand's life.

By knowing who it is, Borrow My Doggy brings its stories to life in different ways. Whether through an inspiring TEDx Talk by its founder (https://www.youtube.com/watch?v=IqewBwv4xyw) or member stories that showcase the vibrancy of its community, each macro and micro story builds onto the brand's identity and purpose.

It's tempting to look at successful examples of brand storytelling and want to jump right into telling your own. However, before you dive into storytelling, you need to define who you are.

Regardless of your industry, size, or whether you are a B2C or B2B company, your brand's mission, values, and personality are the foundation to how you build your brand storytelling strategy and, ultimately, the stories you bring to life.

THE PURPOSE LAW

Every company has a purpose, the ultimate reason for its existence. When you clearly identify your purpose, or as Simon Sinek would call it, your why, defining and communicating who you are and what you are trying to achieve becomes easier—and incredibly powerful.

Not only that, when your purpose is clear, it gives your customers, partners, vendors, and employees a chance to feel like they are a part of a tribe. It gives them a much-needed sense of belonging, thus allowing you to build a movement around your purpose.

Purpose should be the core, the DNA, of a business. And every action of that business should authentically articulate its DNA.

To define your purpose, ask the following questions.

Why Does Your Brand Exist?

The concept for Dollar Shave Club was inspired by both a problem and an opportunity. In 2011, founder Michael Dubin met a friend's father-in-law at a party. The friend's father-in-law had a warehouse filled with razor blades that he wanted to sell. This totally random problem struck a chord with Michael.

You see, Michael had a longstanding frustration with the process of purchasing razor blades. From needing to travel to a store, only to have to chase down a store employee to open what he calls the locked "razor fortress," Michael felt there was an opportunity to improve customer experience and pricing for buyers. With the big brands charging a huge markup, why not mail the razor blades directly to consumers to save them the time, hassle, and money?

Dollar Shave Club launched with a hilarious video titled, "Our Blades Are F***ing Great." The video stars Michael walking through a warehouse delivering a no bullsh*t, slapstick pitch sprinkled with quirky moments. Guest appearances include a toddler, a machete, and a giant teddy bear. The video not only spoke to the company's purpose, but it did so in a way that was unique to Dollar Shave Club. The video generated over 12,000 orders on that day and has since been viewed over 25 million times.[2]

While one viral video makes for a great start, Dollar Shave Club knew that it couldn't stop there. If the company was truly going to improve the customer experience around purchasing razors, Michael knew that it needed to do more than sell. Inspired by the notion of a member's club, Michael branded himself the "Club Pro," a savvy grooming concierge who would answer all the weird and wonderful questions his customers could dream up. In doing this, Michael realized that while there was interest, the average guy didn't know that much about grooming best practices. The company then decided to lead the conversation, with helpful, humorous, wacky content on grooming.

If you look at companies that enjoy long-term success, you will notice that like Dollar Shave Club, their core belief—their purpose—hasn't changed since the company's inception. Even though business strategies change and evolve, the core purpose stays consistent. For example, Ford's purpose is to "open the highways to all mankind"; Southwest Airlines's purpose is to provide affordable transportation to the common person; Walt Disney's purpose is to bring joy to children everywhere; and Coca-Cola's purpose is to inspire happiness.

Serving its purpose, Dollar Shave Club went from a one-man operation to a mega brand. It was eventually acquired by Unilever for $1 billion. However, if you visit Dollar Shave Club's website or social media channels today, you will still see the same spirit and purpose in everything that it does.

What Does Your Brand Stand For?

Your company's purpose will shape your brand's values, as well as its personality and voice. As you start crafting your marketing messages and building relationships with your customers, it becomes critically important to be true to what you stand for and be authentic in everything you say, and most important, everything you do. Younger consumers are increasingly aware of companies' heritage, purpose, and values and use them to decide what brands they want to buy and support.

A company's purpose isn't always about solving a problem or filling a gap in the market. It can be about putting your own unique stamp on an existing category by making a difference. While traveling in Argentina in 2006, TOMS founder Blake Mycoskie discovered the alpargata, the so-called national shoe of the country. Soft, casual, and incredibly comfortable, the canvas shoe was everywhere. Later on this trip, Blake met an American woman in a café who was running a volunteer shoe drive, a concept he was not familiar with. Together, they visited villages where many children were growing up without shoes and better understood the hardships they faced firsthand.

Blake started to realize that maybe his trip to Argentina was destined to be more than just a holiday.

He started by raising money from friends and family to buy shoes for the children, but later realized he could do more. Why not create a for-profit business with products that customers loved, allowing TOMS to give back without requiring donations? To do this, TOMS introduced the world to its take on the alpargata, incredibly comfortable yet fashion-forward slip-on shoes.

With every product you purchase, TOMS helps a person in need. The company started by giving one pair of shoes to a child in need for every pair purchased. Now, the company also gives back through eyewear, offering prescription glasses, or when necessary, medical treatment or sight-saving surgery. TOMS Roasting Co. supports water systems in seven countries where the company sources its coffee beans. The company also uses proceeds from TOMS Bags purchases to provide training for skilled birth attendants, plus vital materials needed to help a woman safely give birth.

TOMS's purpose shines so brightly across everything that it does that it has sparked a global movement. It now formally brands itself as "The One for One® Company."

What Is the Culture You Want to Nurture?

The culture you create internally will have a direct impact on your company's reputation externally. If you think your brand's reputation is made out of the marketing messages you create, think again. Your reputation is what your customers (and partners and employees, for that matter) are saying about you when you are not in the room. And it is very visible when employees are not passionate about the brand they work for.

Tony Hsieh, CEO of Zappos, says: "For individuals, character is destiny. For organizations, culture is destiny." So, as you shape your company's purpose, put as much effort, if not more, into building the right culture. Because no amount of creative marketing will overshadow the lack of a strong culture or create internal and external passion that the right culture can ignite. In some cases, your culture can become your organic marketing.

For Zappos, its purpose is its culture. The company formally defines its purpose as, "To live and deliver WOW!" Its purpose means just as much to its employees as it does to its customers. By creating a culture where employees are happy and passionate about the work that they do, Zappos has been able to attract top talent and set the standard for best-in-class customer service.

A key to Zappos's success has been explicitly defining its 10 core values from which it develops the company's culture, brand, and business strategies:

- Deliver WOW through Service
- Embrace and Drive Change
- Create Fun and a Little Weirdness
- Be Adventurous, Creative, and Open-Minded
- Pursue Growth and Learning
- Build Open and Honest Relationships with Communication
- Build a Positive Team and Family Spirit
- Do More with Less
- Be Passionate and Determined
- Be Humble

While Zappos does very little marketing, the campaigns it does activate are tied back to its culture and values. For example, during a recent Leap Year, Zappos developed a Change.org petition to make Leap Day a national paid holiday and led by example, giving its employees the day off.

Zappos had calculated that by working an extra day during a Leap Year, Americans would spend over 1.5 billion hours in the office. In the average person's lifetime alone, that equates to an extra 90 hours working, for free. Why not, once every four years, enjoy a day off and get those hours back? In addition to the Change.org petition, the company shared stories of how its employees enjoyed their Leap Day off, including two employees who decided to use the day to get married, facilitated by CEO Tony Hsieh, of course.[3]

How Do You Define Your Brand Values?

As Zappos showcases, defining and communicating your values (internally and externally) is critical to executing and living your company's purpose. As you drive toward your goals and grow your business, having a solid list of values that can help guide key decisions (large or small) is extremely helpful. Core values don't have to be all things to all people. Rather, they must be specific and authentic to who you are. They need to demonstrate who you are, not who you want to be.

Chances are, if you are at an established company, you already have your values defined. However, as companies grow and evolve, so do their values. Here are important elements to keep in mind as you shape or reevaluate your values.

1. Don't Dictate: Incorporate Employee Feedback and Insights

For companies working on defining their brand values, Buffer offers a great example. The company's founders, Joel Gascoigne and Leo Widrich, were initially inspired by Zappos, as well as Dale Carnegie's famous book, *How to Win Friends and Influence People*. While Joel and Leo knew that insights from both would factor into Buffer's values, these values wouldn't truly be their own unless employees also had their say.

They decided to send a survey. The exercise allowed employees to articulate the company's culture in their own words. Hugely successful, it identified 7 of the 10 values the company uses:

1. Choose positivity.
2. Default to transparency.
3. Focus on self-improvement.
4. Be a no-ego doer.
5. Listen first, then listen more.
6. Have a bias toward clarity.
7. Make time to reflect.
8. Live smarter, not harder.
9. Show gratitude.
10. Do the right thing.[4]

Buffer's values are shared in a SlideShare presentation, each with four or five supporting bullet points (https://open.buffer.com/creating-values/). Personal language like "you" is used to strike the right chord with employees.

Employee feedback is critical in defining your core values because teams within your company need to understand how your values guide their actions. They need to see that the leadership team is not only passionate about the values, but lives by them and uses them as guiding principles. A company's values should be evident in employees' daily work, their goals, and the interactions they have with others in the business.

2. Stay Grounded in Your Reality

Richard Branson, founder of the Virgin Group, cautions, "Too many companies want their brands to reflect some idealized, perfected image of themselves. As a consequence their brands acquire no texture, no character."[5]

When defining your core values, the key is to be grounded in reality. When building the Virgin Group, Richard Branson acknowledged that the company values were rooted in his strengths and, more important, his weaknesses. Growing up with dyslexia, Branson had a hard time understanding complex topics or jargon. When building the Virgin Group, simplicity became both a core value and a brand differentiator.

"My dyslexia helped us to make all communications across the company efficient. In consequence, Virgin developed a clear-cut, simple way of doing things that became part of our company's culture. This was especially helpful when, say, we launched a bank. Over the years, this approach has enabled us to find paths to simplicity where others might see only complexity. I think we see the big picture and embrace unconventional thinking more easily. I think customers love the Virgin brand because we do not talk above them or talk down to them. We talk to them—and simply," said Branson.[6]

3. **Think Beyond Your Office Walls**

   When defining your values, think beyond your office walls. Ask yourself, do your company's values align with the customer experience that you provide? It's one thing to have values around transparency or doing the right thing, but they mean absolutely nothing if they're not consistent with how your customers perceive your brand.

   Just as Richard Branson observed how many companies shape their values around an aspirational version of themselves, make sure you are not trying to be someone that you are not. If your customer experience is not quite where it needs to be, use the steps and strategies you're taking to fix it as inspiration when setting your values.

4. **Don't Set 'Em and Forget 'Em: Your Values Should Be Continually Evolving**

   Just because you have defined your core values does not mean that you are stuck with them forever. In fact, quite the opposite! Companies continually grow over their lifespan, requiring your core values or mission to evolve to drive new levels of success.

   HubSpot communicates its purpose and values using a deck on its Culture Code, the operating system that powers the company. There have been dozens of versions of the deck, and it has been viewed more than 3.7 million times.[7]

   In the Culture Code, HubSpot has seven core values that it lives by:

   1. We commit maniacally to both our **mission** and **metrics**.

2. We look to the long term and **solve for the customer.**
3. We **share openly** and are **remarkably transparent**.
4. We favor **autonomy** and take **ownership**.
5. We believe our best perk is **amazing people**.
6. We dare to be **different** and question the status quo.
7. We recognize that **life is short**.

Dharmesh Shah, HubSpot's founder and CTO, said, "As a programmer, I believe building culture is a lot like building a product. First, just like with product, you need to talk to your 'customers.' In the case of culture, the 'customers' of the culture are the people that work in the company. Next, just like product, you need to iterate on your code constantly. And even then, the best products are always a work in progress."

In early 2018, Dharmesh found a "bug" in the Culture Code that needed fixing. HubSpot uses HEART—Humble, Effective, Adaptable, Remarkable, and Transparent—to describe qualities it values in its employees. As HubSpot continued to grow and evolve, simply being effective wasn't enough anymore. Dharmesh reflected on the current employee culture, plus some of the hiring mistakes he personally had made, and came to an aha moment. Employees who were just effective weren't top performers. Instead, it was the employees who were empathetic who truly shined, those who genuinely cared about their fellow employees and customers. As a result, HEART now stands for:

Humble, Empathetic, Adaptable, Remarkable, and Transparent.[8]

It may seem like a small change, but the words and values you use have an impact on your business. If your culture and values result in employees feeling empowered and bringing their best selves to work, it can be a powerful differentiator in everything that you do.

THE VISUAL IDENTITY LAW

It's hard to imagine brands like Nike without its iconic swoosh, McDonald's without the golden arches, or Apple without its namesake logo.

However, developing a strong visual identity goes beyond your logo. Every element that goes into your brand, from the colors and fonts to the overall design aesthetics—every image and video—reflects your brand. So much so, that having a strong, consistent visual identity gives your brand a competitive edge in the market. In a time of shrinking attention spans, companies with a strong visual identity are more recognizable, trustworthy, and memorable to customers.

That is the reason why companies invest heavily in building a strong brand identity. Shaping the right visual identity is a powerful differentiator—and a huge detractor if not done correctly.

Gap found this out the hard way in 2010 when it attempted to launch a companywide rebrand to showcase its new, more modern brand identity. The company swapped its iconic navy square logo with GAP in white capital letters for one that spelled out

"Gap" in black with a small blue gradient square over-lapping the upper right side of the "p."

The Internet exploded with negative feedback on the new logo. Customers, design and marketing industry experts, and even the press were quick to jump in with their two cents on every element of the new logo.

On Twitter, one customer set up a parody @GapLogo Twitter account in protest, which collected nearly 5,000 followers. Another individual built a "Make your own Gap logo" site named Craplogo, which went viral, prompting nearly 14,000 parody versions of the Gap logo redesign.

AdAge summed up the majority of the feedback from the design and marketing community: "Helvetica is so overused that it fails to provide a unique visual identifier for any company that chooses it as its logo. But even if you forget about all of that, why would Gap choose the same typeface as one of its main competitors, American Apparel, who use Helvetica for its hipster irony and expressionless detachment similar to that of its models? To stand apart and move into the twenty-first century convincingly, Gap should have chosen something less generic and with a tad more personality. The square gradient is unfortunate because it's completely gratuitous, like an asterisk at the end of a word, except there is no footnote. Or, in other words, there is no there there. Just a vapid reminder that the word Gap used to live within a blue square in its previous incarnation."[9]

Marka Hansen, president of Gap North America at the time of the rebrand, said, "We've been listening to and watching all of the comments this past week. We heard them say over and over again they are passionate about our blue box logo, and they want it back. So we've made the decision to do just that—we will bring it back across all channels."[10]

The crazy thing? Gap's rebrand fail reportedly cost the company $100 million.[11]

The key lesson here? Whether you are an established company or one that is just starting out, your visual brand identity matters. It is your definitive signature and an opportunity to humanize the story of your brand. However, learn from Gap's mistakes. Your visual identity should reflect who you truly are and the experience that you deliver through your company. If you treat it like a shortcut or try to present yourself as someone you are not, you will not be successful.

If you are an established company, chances are you already have gone through a painstaking process to develop and define your visual brand identity. You likely have a massive brand guidelines book, complete with your logo, brand colors, and dos and don'ts for how designers and marketers can use various brand elements across customer touchpoints.

If that is the case, fret not, because we're not here to blow up your brand. In fact, we would encourage you to dig further into how your brand was built, from your logo and the colors you use, to what your company is looking to convey through its visual identity and how your brand identity has evolved over the years. More often than not, the story behind your visual identity can be quite compelling, influencing both the macro and micro stories that you tell.

However, if you are a newer business looking to build or further enhance your visual identity, start by reflecting on the work you have done previously in this chapter on knowing who you are. By knowing who you are as a brand, you can start the creative process of how you can express your story, purpose, values, and culture in your visual style.

For example, the colors you select to represent your brand reveal a lot about you. Choose them wisely. Research shows that 60 percent of people decide if they are attracted or not to a message based on what color it is. Furthermore, having well-defined, consistent colors associated with your brand can actually increase brand recognition up to 80 percent.[12]

The Logo Company, a company that—you guessed it—exists purely to design logos for businesses, has done extensive research on the different emotions and personality traits that different colors reflect.

Here are some popular colors and what they symbolize:

- Yellow: optimism, clarity, warmth
- Orange: friendly, cheerful, confident
- Red: excitement, bold, youthful
- Purple: creative, wise, imaginative
- Blue: trust, strength, dependable
- Green: peaceful, growth, health
- Gray: balance, neutral, calm[13]

When we were writing and developing the visual identity for our first book, *The Power of Visual Storytelling*, we gravitated toward red. As we wrote this book and built the supporting assets for our brand, like our website, we knew that it had to be red. We want this book to be exciting and bold. And if we can inspire you with our strategies and tips, we hope you will have a burst of energy to carry you through developing your brand storytelling efforts!

Some companies that are partial to the color red include Target, Coca-Cola, and Netflix. In contrast, iconic technology brands such as Dell, IBM, Intel, and GE leverage blue's strong, trustworthy persona to represent their brands. It's also easy to see why brands such as Whole Foods, Starbucks, and Girl Scouts use green to showcase a peaceful, healthful brand identity.

Shaping a strong visual identity is just a start. The fun comes from how you activate it to tell your brand story.

For example, when I (Ekaterina) led Intel's efforts in building and nurturing its communities on social media channels, my team made the conscious decision to add a consistent visual background to our images; that element was the processor wafer, a mix of blues, yellows, oranges, and reds.

The processor wafer has a very recognizable hue that is familiar to folks in the industry. By using this element the company left an indelible brand footprint on every visual in a subtle way. That visual consistency made brand assets recognizable across channels and conversations and eliminated the need for in-your-face branding.

At Dunkin' Donuts, my (Jessica's) colleagues and I sought inspiration not just from the brand colors, but also the iconic double Ds. On social media, our team would look for playful ways to incorporate the DDs into copy, whether it was an official brand post or a one-to-one response. For example, when a fan tweeted, "Yesterday, I was with friends @DunkinDonuts #loveit #best #donuts #on #earth!" Dunkin' responded with, "AgreeDD! Dunkin' Donuts IS the best place on earth, but we're also biased :)."

The goal? Showcase the brand's playful, upbeat personality with a small unexpected touch. The brand's iconic DDs played an important role on one of Dunkin'

Donuts's most important days, its IPO. Dunkin' asked NASDAQ if it would consider altering its logo on the day of the IPO. Much to the company's surprise—and delight—NASDAQ loved the idea and changed its logo on all digital channels, from its website to screens in New York City's Times Square, to "NAS**DD**AQ" for the day. Naturally, the "Ds" were in orange and pink to reflect Dunkin's logo.

As you can see from these examples, there are many important elements that form a brand's visual identity. For the purposes of this book, we won't go into further depth. After all, there are plenty of great books dedicated to the topic. What we want to stress, however, is that knowing your company's history, purpose, and identity will help you uncover and bring to life the coolest stories.

THE DIFFERENTIATION LAW

Imagine this. You're walking down the street, and a man pops out of his car. At first glance, he looks like your average man in a blazer, shirt, and tie. However, upon a closer look, you realize that he is wearing his traditional blazer with tight jean shorts and sky-high stiletto heels.

He proceeds to strut his way down the street to The Pussycat Dolls' iconic song, "Don't Cha," pausing strategically to burst into impressive dance moves. Naturally, there is an admirable derriere and twerking involved. As the passerby on the street watch the scene unfold, some are entertained, while others are shocked.

What on earth is this man doing? And why?

The man's name is Dave, and he is doing his version of the epic strut (#EpicStrut), a victory dance like no other that celebrates the great feeling of saving money.[14]

The scene we just described can be observed in a hilarious video courtesy of Moneysupermarket.com, a price comparison website in the United Kingdom that helps consumers save money across banks, insurers, credit cards, energy suppliers, and more (https://www.youtube.com/watch?v=DaP9sN67QKI).

The video quickly took the United Kingdom by storm. It became the number one trending topic on Twitter, was parodied numerous times, and Dave became a sought-after guest on the top morning TV shows to answer hard-hitting questions like, "Is your backside . . . real?"

Moneysupermarket.com estimated that it generated 10 million pounds worth of free advertising as a result of the numerous parodies and TV appearances. But it didn't just stop there. Dave became a popular costume for bachelor parties, with men dressing up like him and hitting the town.[15]

The epic success of Moneysupermarket.com's campaign and subsequent campaigns featuring a pole-dancing construction worker (yes, really) resulted in £50 million in revenue growth. Dave's #EpicStrut was also named the United Kingdom's top 2015 campaign.

Here are some brand differentiation tips.

Work Your Top Assets

While it's clear that the more outrageous and gimmicky elements of Moneysupermarket.com's campaigns skyrocketed it to success, the important takeaway here is that the company is working its top assets and key differentiators—both literally and figuratively.

Moneysupermarket.com's mission is to help consumers feel good about saving, managing, and growing their money. The company is also independently run, versus being owned by an insurance company, and believes this makes it even more focused on helping its customers achieve their goals.

We are not recommending that every company boldly strut and twerk its way into its customers' hearts like Moneysupermarket.com. However, by creatively playing to its strengths in a bold and entertaining way, Moneysupermarket.com is not only telling a great story around its key differentiator, but the effort helped propel its business to new levels.

This is precisely why you need to spend some time analyzing your top assets compared to those of your competitors.

Start by asking yourself, what makes your company unique?

- Your company culture
- Your purpose and mission
- Your brand personality
- Your customers
- Your involvement in the community and corporate social responsibility programs
- Your employees and executives
- Your niche communities or ecosystem around your brand
- Your products and services

From there, dig a bit deeper into your differentiators. Moneysupermarket.com plays off of its brand personality and its product's value proposition of saving customers money. However, your key differentiators could be the unique elements that are found in your product or a special method you use to make them. It could be the incredible customer service you provide. Or perhaps you've scored a coveted award or endorsements from respected industry groups. Exploring each of these elements forces you to think creatively about your brand's "magic," and how you can harness its power to stand out from your competitors.

A word of caution: when identifying your key differentiators, do not default to focusing on your products and services. In doing so, you are limiting your brand storytelling potential. The brands that truly double down on what makes them unique are the ones that carve out valuable niches in the market—and in their customers' minds.

Remember that your opinion is not the only one that matters. Do your customers believe those assets and differentiators to be true? Which ones will resonate the most with them?

Ask yourself how your key differentiators:

- Solve a customer's problem
- Fulfill a customer's needs or wants
- Add value to your customers' lives
- Create a positive customer experience

In many industries, consumers have more choices than ever before and are hardwired to seek out the best or the most relevant products or services to meet their needs and wants. Make sure you are aligned with your customers and have proof points to back up your key differentiators as you shape them into inspiring macro and micro brand stories.

Your Vibe Attracts Your Tribe

Moneysupermarket.com's #EpicStrut was recognized as the United Kingdom's top campaign of 2015 and struck a chord with a large audience of cheeky Brits. From sassy dance moves to Dave's over-the-top ensemble, Moneysupermarket.com knew that the ad would make an impression. However, it couldn't have predicted that Dave would become an overnight sensation.

As evidenced by numerous parody videos and groups of men dressing up as Dave for their "stag dos," or bachelor parties as they're called in the United States, the success of this campaign and its oh-so-sassy main character highlights a critical point: your vibe attracts your tribe.

It's not just about the products and services you sell. Your brand personality, from your tone of voice to the campaigns and stories you share about your best assets and key differentiators, determines the types of customers you attract and retain, as well as the experiences you provide them. As a result, companies must focus on how their stories resonate with their target audience. Your target audience is your tribe, and they are the ones who matter.

Writer and motivational speaker Jay Danzie captured it perfectly when he said, "Your smile is your logo, your personality is your business card, how you leave others feeling after having an experience with you becomes your trademark."[16]

The question then becomes, how do you want your customers to experience your brand? And how do you want your customers to perceive you? Are you lighthearted, funny, serious, humble, geeky, or inspirational? The personality you project will be reflected across every element of your business, from how you speak to customers to how you position your products and services in the marketplace.

With its iconic slogan, "Just do it," Nike positions its brand personality as "the sporting warrior." Its key differentiator is its best-in-class sports apparel and footwear, trusted by top professional and amateur athletes around the world. The company uses its sporting warrior persona to reach every athlete in the world, calling out, "If you have a body, you are an athlete." The company's campaigns also reflect Nike's passion for its community of athletes. For example, in the "Your Year with Nike+" campaign, the company and its agency AKQA created over 100,000 personalized one-minute animated films for its most active Nike+ users. The goal was to celebrate a strong year by bringing each customer's Nike+ performance data to life, while inspiring its most active users to keep working hard and achieve better results the following year.[17]

Alternatively, KFC's brand personality is centered around infusing humor with heritage. Since it was founded in 1930 in Kentucky, the Colonel has been KFC's brand ambassador, with various famous faces bringing his fun-loving character to life. To this day, KFC uses its founder's original recipe of 11 herbs and spices, so the brand does wacky things like following only 11 people on Twitter. More specifically, 11 herbs and spices: five Spice Girls and six guys named Herb. When one fan finally noticed and made the story public, KFC commissioned a custom painting of him enjoying a piggyback ride from the Colonel, with a chicken drumstick in hand (of course). As a result of its quirky and humorous brand persona, KFC keeps its fans wondering what juicy tidbit could fall into their laps or feeds next, whether it's a romantic novel launched just in time for Mother's Day appropriately called Tender Wings of Desire or a chicken wing box that doubles as a drone.

If you're a B2B brand marketer reading this, we hope you're not thinking, "Oh, c'mon, consumer brands always have more fun." Nope! It's not just consumer brands that can shape and bring exciting brand personalities to life. There is absolutely no reason why B2B brands cannot celebrate their key differentiators and express their unique personalities.

For example, Voxbone, a CaaS or Communications as a Service company, aims to push the boundaries of cloud telephony. Chances are, if you've dialed into a conference call, received a text update from an on-demand car service, or spoken with an international customer support team, there is a good chance you have used Voxbone's services.

Voxbone's passion and mission is to provide global companies with "strangely simple communications" through its products and services, but also through its messaging. The company infuses this mission with an "SaaS-minded AND sassy" personality across all of its customer touchpoints, from calling its employees "The Untanglers," to describing its product features as "Gloriously Global," "Kick-Ass Quality," and "Trusted by Unicorns and Giants Alike." By bringing a quirky yet whip-smart brand to the table, Voxbone is successfully raising greater awareness for what it does, making the sales cycle much more fun and enabling the company to differentiate itself and grow its tribe of loyal customers who appreciate and relate to who it is.

Your Size Doesn't Matter

While we mostly use large brand examples throughout the book, the reality is that anyone can follow the principles and guidelines we've outlined. Whether you are a small business or a personal brand, most principles will apply to you, as the following story illustrates.

Jala Smith-Huys, founder of Seek & Swoon, created a business that stands out. Seek & Swoon creates and sells knit throw blankets inspired by a love of design, home goods, and travel (Figure 1.1).

FIGURE 1.1   Seek & Swoon's home page

Seek & Swoon differentiates itself in three ways:

- Jala's designs are her own. They are inspired not only by the places she and her family travel to but by our world—taking care of it, exploring it, and adding to its beauty.

- The blankets are made in the United States in partnership with a family-run knitting mill (one of the few left in the country).
- Eco throws are made from recycled materials.

The best part about the company is that Seek & Swoon isn't just about throws. "My story is about warmth, cuddling, travel, exploration, wanderlust, sustainability, small batch, American made, and supporting local," Jala told us in an interview. "When you have a house guest and they're drawn to the throw on your couch, it's not just a throw that's made in China by somebody. It's a throw inspired by a beautiful place, made by a designer in Portland, Oregon, who's partnered with a family-owned US mill to knit her throws from recycled cotton. I think this also puts some pride around the purchase because, as a consumer, you know you're supporting two small businesses (Seek & Swoon and the mill), you're contributing to efforts that prevent waste from going into the landfill (recycled cotton), and design patterns are aspirational because they inspire adventure and the exploration of our planet."

When Jala tells people about Seek & Swoon, whether it is a potential wholesale partner, customer, or journalist, all are initially drawn in by the story more than the product. "There's a significant difference in reaction between when I say, 'I design cotton throws,' and when I add, 'They're made at an American family-owned mill from recycled cotton and inspired by beautiful places around the world,'" she says, "That's when the aha moment happens." The story gives her a North Star to orient her designs and her marketing content to, she adds.

These brand differentiators are interesting and important to people from 25 to 55 who want to support small businesses, believe in protecting the planet and being part of the solution, and daydream about travel, vacations, and new places that make them feel alive.

As Jala continued to connect to a new audience through the expansion of her offerings (baby blankets and custom wedding throws), she stayed true to her brand message and brand purpose.

"The Seek & Swoon story is really at the heart of everything I do," Jala says passionately. "It drives the type of retailers I wholesale to, the vendors that I partner with, and, of course, the designs of the throws themselves. And for as long as I travel and see this world, whether it be two hours to the Oregon coast or two days to Australia, there will always be a throw for me to design."

Call it a story. Call it DNA. Or call it heart. Whatever you call it, customers can feel authenticity miles away. And that, in itself, is a key differentiator.

THE AUTHENTICITY LAW

Like most women in commercials, we like to start each morning by doing yoga in our designer sportswear, journaling in a fancy notebook, and eating a wholesome, farm fresh breakfast. Naturally, we have loads and loads of free time, can carefully select the perfect outfit, and artfully style our hair and makeup.

Because, you know, that's real life.

Frustrated by how most companies market to women, Organic Valley, a consumer packaged goods company that sells organic food and beverages, knew that it needed to break the mold, both in its product line and in how it speaks to its customers.

The company conducted a survey of 1,000 women between the ages of 25 and 54 and found that:

- 57 percent of women are up before the sun rises
- 21 percent of women check their work e-mail before getting out of bed
- 9 percent of women cite dry shampoo as one of the greatest inventions of the twentieth century
- 33 percent of women never make their bed
- 21 percent of women have used an article of clothing to camouflage a stain
- 58 percent of women will swear at someone or something over the course of their day
- 16 percent of women would describe their morning with the hashtag #blessed

What Organic Valley discovered is that most women's mornings, and days, for that matter, are "officially cray." From messy houses to kids and families to take care of, many women are lucky if they have a few minutes to themselves, let alone time to eat breakfast.

Organic Valley channeled these insights into a brand storytelling campaign called the "Real Morning Report" and brought them to life in a brutally honest, yet humorous video to promote its new Organic Balance Protein Shake, a delicious breakfast for busy women. It's worth watching: https://www.youtube.com/watch?time_continue=91&v=bh19YxASA-4. It's sweet and messy and beautiful and real. And no, we did not tear up when we watched it. It was allergies.

If research and customer insights paint a very specific picture, then why do so many companies still sell an unachievable, aspirational dream to their customers? Not only is it inauthentic, it showcases a lack of understanding and empathy for your customers. Simply, it lacks humanity.

Moreover, it goes beyond a brand being perceived as "out of touch" or a marketing campaign that "missed the mark." A lack of authenticity has become the proverbial Achilles' heel for brands. Research from Stackla shows that 86 percent of people say authenticity is important when deciding what brands they like and support. The challenge? Only 57 percent of people perceive content from brands as authentic.[18]

As a result, it has never been more important for companies to truly ask themselves, how do we ensure authenticity in everything that we do?

Develop a Brand Authenticity Playbook™

To ensure that the word *authentic* becomes more than just a buzzword for your company, create what we call an Authenticity Playbook.

Here's why. What authenticity means for your company can be hard to define. Too often, companies default to using their brand guidelines and values as their definition of authenticity. While these elements are valuable and a good place to start, they also tend to be rigid and not reflective of the real-time nature of how customers interact with businesses today.

An Authenticity Playbook takes your brand guidelines to the next level; it needs to be treated as an extension of them. Brand guidelines are typically reflective of your brand image and style, containing information on how to use your colors and logo, as well as your tone of voice and mission. While these elements are all valuable in their own right, they don't delve deeply enough into what truly defines your brand's character.

An Authenticity Playbook allows you to identify and create a framework, plus key themes and examples of how your brand can build trust and respect with your current and prospective customer base. In today's business climate, your customers believe that actions speak louder than words. As a result, your Authenticity Playbook needs to be shaped around what issues your company stands for across all lines of your business, from how you source your products and treat your employees to key political issues, and more.

To create an Authenticity Playbook personalized to your company, we recommend going through the process of brainstorming what is important to your brand. Go through the many scenarios and issues that your company could be pulled into and think strategically about how you want your company to be perceived. Then take it a step further. Align your Authenticity Playbook with your company's internal and external messaging (public relations, customer service, sales training, annual reports, etc.), plus your crisis management planning. The more integrated this messaging is across your company, the more consistent it will be across all your external customer touchpoints.

An Authenticity Playbook should be honest and aligned with your brand mission and values. It should include (but not be limited to):

- Your brand authority and what differentiates you from others in your industry
- Your company's founding principles and how they have evolved over time
- The why behind how your run your business (sourcing products, supply chain, operations, employee guidelines and treatment, corporate social responsibility policies)
- Your stance on important issues (social, political, environmental)
- Your key stakeholders and how your actions, values, and voice will shape their perception of you—customers, employees, investors, the news media, industry influencers, activist and special interest groups, and more
- Your "customer delight" approach across the organization

The beauty of the Authenticity Playbook is that it is unique to every company. The content of the playbook should be defined by what you think is important to your brand as a citizen of the world. It is your opportunity to humanize your brand. Go beyond your logo and show people your strength of character as a company.

The Power of Authenticity and Depositing Social Capital

The reason an Authenticity Playbook matters is that while it's easy to say "Be real! Stay true to your brand personality!" it can be challenging for companies to define what it means in the context of your brand. An Authenticity Playbook helps you identify these important elements so you can then build the subsequent strategies and processes to ensure consistency and grow your brand's social capital.

According to Kathleen Hall, corporate vice president of brand, advertising, and research at Microsoft, "You need to be principle based and values based. When you become inauthentic you try to make a statement but it's not true to who you are and what you are about, so you're obviously trying to capitalize on the situation. You can't really borrow from social capital. You have to deposit into it."[19]

Creating an Authenticity Playbook is also a good exercise for identifying potential weaknesses that are holding your company back. For example, it could be that your company has been stuck on a specific persona based on who you want to be, versus who you really are, which may be significantly different.

It's worth noting that an Authenticity Playbook is not just about the big picture. It also allows you to identify inconsistencies. Once you have a robust Authenticity Playbook, your focus can shift to consistency and refinement.

For example, the customer service team for UK grocery store chain Tesco has earned a reputation for infusing humor into its communications with customers. When a customer complained about purchasing a hollow Scotch Egg (a British favorite consisting of a hard-boiled egg wrapped in sausage meat, coated in breadcrumbs, and fried), saying that it looked like it was "laughing at her," Tesco's team sent her back a brilliant response.

The team posted a personalized poem on its Facebook page that read, "O Egg, egg, wherefore art thou, egg? Deny thy breadcrumbs and refuse thy sausage meat, or if thou wilt not, be but sworn my love and I'll no longer be a scotch egg eater. Shall I hear more, or shall I speak at this? 'Tis by thy snack that is my enemy: thou art thyself, though not a scotch egg eater no more."[20]

The customer service rep continued, "I'm terribly sorry about the missing egg, what a crime against nature! I don't think that it's laughing at you, I think it's screaming, 'WHERE'S MY EGG!!!' I would like to make the supplier aware of this and refund you, can you please Private Message me the following . . ."[21]

While it's frustrating to buy a faulty product, it's hard not to feel better about it after reading this customer response from Tesco. It hits all the right notes—humor, honesty, and humility—all while solving her problem.

This example follows a long line of clever customer service wins from Tesco. They have had a ripple effect, prompting other customers to put a bit of creativity into their customer service complaints in hopes of a witty response from Tesco. A customer who found a dead worm in his cucumber invited the company to the worm's backyard funeral, prompting Tesco to send a sympathy card with a poem.

While the strategy is both brilliant and authentic, here's the rub: it doesn't extend beyond the customer service team! Tesco's funny responses continue to drive public relations wins for the company, and customers love hearing about them, yet the brand defaults to sharing only content about the products it sells. Why not incorporate this playful spirit into more magical stories that go beyond their products?

Every response, promise, and interaction can and will be judged in the court of customer perception.

If you truly want to build highly engaged customer tribes, remember that your brand needs to be consistent. Companies that consistently embrace authenticity and transparency across all their customer touchpoints uncover something powerful: their customers will do the marketing for them.

Speaking of walking the talk, this brings us to the Conflict Law. This is where you really get a chance to show the world what you stand for—in action.

THE CONFLICT LAW

On March 10, 2014, Honey Maid, a brand that makes graham crackers, launched its "This Is Wholesome" campaign to celebrate the many different types of families. The campaign video opens on a family with two dads, one of whom is feeding a baby while the other lovingly kisses the baby on the head, before panning to a family with a mom, dad, and young daughter rocking out to her father playing the drums. As various types of families enjoying time together flash across the screen, from single parent to multiracial and military families, a narrator says, "No matter how things change, what makes us wholesome never will. Honey Maid: everyday wholesome snacks for every wholesome family. This is wholesome."[22] Watch the full video here: https://www.youtube.com/watch?v= 2xeanX6xnRU.

The inspiration for the campaign came from the brand's wholesome heritage and the families who purchase Honey Maid's products. Honey Maid had realized that the brand's ads featuring a "wholesome family" were not reflective of the makeup of modern-day families in the United States, let alone the company's customers. It was time to take a stand and celebrate the new normal for families.

However, in order to truly take a stand and update the brand, Gary Osifchin, senior marketing director for Honey Maid, knew that it needed to be more than a one-off campaign, noting, "I had these conversations internally with senior management from the start, that said if we decide to do this, first we're always going to tell our stories the right way, and secondly we're always going to be telling these stories. Deciding to do it out of the gate meant deciding to go on a journey of reinventing the brand. We were going to stick with the stories representing some of the breadth and depth that exists in America. We can't represent everyone, but we do represent some of the diversity in America today."[23]

It was just as important to show the authenticity of the families featured. Gary continued, "What's been so important is to always show up in a very honest, authentic way. The families are all real families, and we're on this journey to always tell real stories. The juxtaposition of that with the enjoyment of our Honey Maid products works together nicely. It's a simple story that we're telling. That's part of the magic that works so well for us."[24]

Honey Maid launched the campaign across traditional, digital, and social media, also leveraging a tool called Thunderclap, which allows users to schedule and amplify certain messages on a specific date and time for a greater chance of awareness. The message for the Thunderclap read, "No matter how families change, what makes them wholesome never will. Help me share this message #thisiswholesome http://thndr.it/1i4MCUu."[25]

Suffice it to say, the campaign struck a chord. As expected, not everyone was happy. Conservative activist groups like One Million Moms were quick to rally against Honey Maid. The group launched a letter-writing campaign against the company, stating, "Nabisco should be ashamed of themselves for their latest Honey Maid and Teddy Graham cracker commercial where they attempt to normalize sin. This commercial not only promotes homosexuality, but then calls the scene in the advertisement wholesome."[26]

The backlash was to be expected. But what we didn't expect was the elegant and absolutely sublime way the company responded. It didn't fold. It didn't back down. Instead, it released another video. This simple, yet powerful response is one of the best pieces of marketing we have ever seen. Watch it right now: https://www.youtube.com/watch?v=cBC-pRFt9OM. We'll wait.

The video starts with "On March 10, 2014, Honey Maid launched 'This Is Wholesome,' a commercial that celebrates all families. Some people didn't agree with our message." Then it shows a sample of negative comments the company received, such as "Horrible," "NOT 'WHOLESOME'" and "Disgusting!!" The video message continues: "So we asked two artists to take the negative comments and turn them into something else." You then see the artists Linsey Burritt and Crystal Grover taking a printout of each hateful comment, rolling it into a tube, and then putting the tubes together in a sculpture-like assemblage that spells out the word "Love." As the artists leave the scene, you see the following message: "But the best part was all the positive messages we received. Over ten times as many." Then suddenly the rest of the room (the space around the "Love" sculpture) fills up with tubes that hold positive messages the company received, such as "family is family," "makes my heart happy," and "most beautiful thing." And the final message: "Proving that only one thing really matters when it comes to family . . . ," and the camera zooms out to show the roomful of paper tubes at the center of which is the word "Love."

The halo effect of the original campaign, plus follow-up campaigns and stories about modern families, has been powerful. As Gary Osifchin said, "It's catapulted the brand to the emotional level. Historically, the brand's always been used in recipes, but we've gone from that to a brand that people want and choose to use because of the message we're putting into the world." The message the company truly believes. The message it stands behind.

The New Yorker said it shows how things have changed "in the most radical and moving way of any national campaign so far."[27]

Should your company take a stand? Let's try to answer that question by looking at the heights and pitfalls companies experience when standing up for what they believe in.

Don't Be Switzerland: Brands Have More to Lose by Staying Silent Than by Speaking Out

Look closer at companies like TOMS, Airbnb, and Patagonia, and it is easy to see the power and opportunity to differentiate your brand by taking a stand for what you believe in. As society and consumer demand for transparency evolve, companies that take a stand are quickly becoming the norm and not the outliers. So much so that companies that are not willing to share what they stand for run the risk of losing customers.

Case in point: Sprout Social's report "Championing Change in the Age of Social Media" reveals that consumers want brands to understand a company's stance on issues that are important to them. Two-thirds of consumers say it is important for brands to take a public stance on social and political issues, while 58 percent are open to hearing about a company's stance via social media.[28]

A good example is Airbnb's #WeAccept campaign. The campaign was created on short notice in response to President Donald Trump's travel ban and stars its employees. In the video, the camera zooms in on the diverse faces of Airbnb's employees as we hear, "We believe no matter who you are, where you're from, who you love, or who you worship, we all belong. The world is more beautiful the more you accept. #WeAccept."[29]

Given that the Super Bowl was just days away, the company decided to take the plunge and purchase a 30-second spot to run the video during the game for maximum awareness. The #WeAccept campaign included a letter from Airbnb's founders featured on its website, plus social media content featuring personal stories from its employees: https://www.airbnb.co .uk/weaccept.

The letter states, "We know this is an idealistic notion that faces huge obstacles because of something that also seems simple, but isn't—that not everyone is accepted."[30]

The letter then goes on to showcase Airbnb's goal of providing short-term housing to over 100,000 people in need over the next five years, including refugees, disaster survivors, and relief workers.

Airbnb's stance, combined with the quality of its message and timing, resulted in #WeAccept becoming the most tweeted hashtag during Super Bowl LI, with over 33,000 tweets and 87 million earned impressions. It was covered by 60 global news outlets, crediting Airbnb for not only making a bold statement, but for creating a strong call to action for its community to join in and help. Airbnb continues to document its progress on its website, citing more than 15,000 of its members volunteering to donate their homes and over $4 million raised for the International Rescue Committee.[31]

While taking a stand on political issues is often a slippery slope, what made Airbnb's response well received is that it is aligned with the company's mission. Airbnb's mission is "to create a world where people can belong when they travel by being connected to local cultures and having unique travel experiences."[32] Combined with the company's continued commitment to providing emergency housing during global disasters, it's easy to understand that Airbnb would advocate for the rights of refugees, survivors, and relief workers.

Furthermore, #WeAccept reinforces the type of customer and community Airbnb has and will continue to build. When you take a stand as a company, you will not appeal to everyone. However, if you deeply understand your core customer base and align your stance with issues that are meaningful to them, that is where the magic happens. By acting on what it believed in, Airbnb made its existing customers proud and attracted a group of like-minded customers to join its tribe.

Align Advocacy with Your Authenticity Playbook

Whether you are a local, national, or global business, having a deep understanding of where your company stands on issues of importance to your business and to your customers has never been more important.

Earlier in this chapter, we put you through a boot camp of sorts. By delving into who you are, your purpose, brand values, and key differentiators, and developing an Authenticity Playbook, you have built a solid foundation that will inform how, when, and on what topics your brand should take a stance.

In Sprout Social's report "Championing Change in the Age of Social Media," the company uncovered that relevance is key to reception. Forty-seven percent of consumers say brands are most credible when an issue directly impacts their customers, while 40 percent see credibility in issues impacting employees and 30 percent in business operations.[33]

A compelling example comes from GE, whose mission is to advocate and solve for the talent crisis for women in STEM (science, technology, engineering, and mathematics) roles. In 2017, GE announced that it would lead by example, publicly sharing its goals of having 20,000 women fill STEM roles by 2020 and obtaining 50:50 representation for its technical entry-level programs.[34]

While GE's stance is admirable, what truly made it a home run is the fact that the company has data to back up its mission. GE's research shows that the current percentage of women in engineering and IT careers is only 14 and 25 percent respectively in the United States. Although women make up 55 percent of all college and graduate students overall, only 18 percent of computer science graduates are female. If these numbers do not increase among women, companies like GE will not have a large enough pipeline of talent to meet their future hiring and business growth needs.[35]

In addition to a white paper and press release, GE created a thought-provoking campaign to bring this issue to life by posing the question, "What if we treated great female scientists like celebrities?" The campaign stars Millie Dresselhaus, the first woman to win the National Medal of Science in Engineering and a life-long pioneer and champion for more women to pursue careers in science.

The campaign imagines a world where Millie is treated like a celebrity. From Millie Dresselhaus dolls to women copying her look and being followed constantly by the paparazzi, the campaign asserts that the real celebrities are the ones with incredible achievements and contributions to society: https://www.youtube.com/watch?time_continue=21&v=sQ6_fOX7lTQ.

"We think that celebrating people, in this case women, who have had great achievements is far more important than celebrating people who are famous for fame's sake," said Linda Boff, GE's chief marketing officer. "There are people out there—Millie Dresselhaus is the one we've chosen to highlight—who have done remarkable things and deserve admiration and adulation, and holding up those women as role models is a really fun way to shine a light on what we're calling balancing the equation and addressing what is this industry-wide challenge of getting more women in STEM."[36]

The campaign launched on February 8, 2017, just 12 days before Millie Dresselhaus passed away at age 86. The GE campaign was but one element of her incredibly successful career, which included being the first female faculty member at the Massachusetts Institute of Technology (MIT), cowriting eight books, publishing more than 1,700 scientific papers, winning numerous accolades and awards, and serving in leadership roles on numerous societies, such as the American Physical Society and the American Association for the Advancement of Science. She even earned the nickname "The Queen of Carbon" among her peers for her contributions and willingness to study "the hardest substance known."[37]

Despite an incredible career and contributions to science, how had we not heard about Millie Dresselhaus before, let alone the other amazing women out there like her?

This is precisely why GE's campaign works. It is a company that is passionate about science, technology, engineering, and mathematics, and this campaign and initiative speak authentically to who GE is as a brand, while highlighting its key differentiator: GE is working on balancing the equation.

The main reason why companies get into trouble when taking a stance on political or societal issues comes from not being true to who they are. Strong brands are unique and see the world through a different lens—their own.

You're Not a Sidewalk:
Don't Let Others Walk All Over You

It started innocently. Every year, Reese's Peanut Butter Cups comes out with tree-shaped candies for the holiday season. Who doesn't love a festive excuse to indulge in one of their favorite treats?

Unfortunately for Reese's, consumers didn't think the treat resembled a tree. They took to social media, sharing photos of their misshapen trees with comments like:

> "Does this look like a Christmas tree to you??"[38]
>
> "#Reeses you call it a tree. I think the rest of us see it as a turd."[39]
>
> "Getting in the Christmas spirit with my . . . Oh wait it's a blob #ReesesChristmasTrees #reesesfail #stilltastesgood"[40]

With consumer conversations about the misshapen trees reaching fever pitch on social media, Reese's addressed its critics in a clever way with content proclaiming #AllTreesAreBeautiful.

The company created a series of visuals of its intended and misshapen trees, paired across festive holiday and winter activities, with lines like:

> "REESE'S celebrates trees of all shapes and sizes. It's not what it looks like, it's what it tastes like."[41]
>
> "Woke up like this. #ThankYou #AllTreesAreBeautiful"[42]
>
> "They look just like their father. #AllTreesAreBeautiful"[43]

While extremely clever, Reese's didn't stop there. The company also responded directly to consumers who tweeted about their misshapen trees with fun and playful replies, such as, "If you keep staring at it we swear it will start to look like a tree. Or you could just eat it. #AllTreesAreBeautiful"[44]

What started as a festive faux pas turned into a customer engagement win.

Not only did Reese's strategy work, it prompted its passionate customer base to jump to its defense and share images of the misshapen trees with messages like, "I love my REESES tree. It tastes wonderful no matter what the shape. ♥ #AllTreesAreBeautiful"[45]

If you learn one thing from Reese's approach, it's this: if you feel strongly about something, don't jump straight into an apology! Make sure you thoroughly analyze the situation and understand if an apology is necessary or if there is wiggle room to be more bold or playful.

We completely understand that it's easy to default to an apology in these situations, and sometimes you absolutely have to. However, had Reese's gone down this path, the story would have been covered differently and potentially discouraged consumer purchases. Instead, the company was smart to take a step back, assess the situation, and take a creative approach to address it. Its general response acknowledges the misshapen trees, and its 1:1 responses speak to their value proposition—the same delicious Reese's Peanut Butter Cup taste that consumers love. As a result, Reese's changed the story while generating positive engagement with its customers.

But how do you know when to stand up for yourself? It comes down to auditing the situation thoroughly. Reese's had done its homework and saw a key theme kept popping up with the customer complaints—that the candy was still delicious. The only thing wrong with the product was its shape. Despite customers poking a little fun at the brand, they were still eating the product. This was precisely the insight Reese's needed to help customers "get their priorities straight" in a fun and playful way.

By standing up for itself, Reese's generated an additional $3 million in sales of its tree-shaped peanut butter cups that year, $1 million of which was in the week leading up to Christmas. The initiative generated one billion earned impressions, 82 percent of which mentioned the company by name.[46]

Talk about polishing a turd!

Whether it's celebrating the new normal for families, taking a stand against discrimination, or vowing to balance the ratio of men and women in STEM, companies must take a stand on the issues of the day that relate to their brand.

However, the big issues of the day are not the only ones that matter. Each and every day, brands like Reese's are faced with a barrage of messages and opportunities to share their opinion or stand up for their point of view. It just comes down to selecting the right ones.

Gone are the days where staying neutral advances or protects your brand. Your brand can no longer afford to be a bystander. Being bold means understanding who you are and what your brand believes is worth fighting for. Brands have a powerful opportunity to make a difference, raise awareness and funds for important issues they believe in,

and ultimately, help to make a positive impact—
at scale.

**Your question shouldn't be "How much
risk are we taking?" It should be "What
is the risk of NOT taking action?"**

Chapter 2

THE STRATEGY LAWS

UNDERSTAND YOUR GOALS

Before we jump into the fun stuff, content creation and distribution, let's talk about the critical step that precedes it: strategy.

Your strategy is what charts your course and gives your company something to rally behind. A well-defined strategy allows your organization and its teams to focus on the right actions and initiatives, saving the company time and money. Your strategy paints the bigger picture and aligns your business objectives.

Why is it important? Too often companies equate storytelling with content. They get caught up in producing a stream of content without considering the bigger picture and brand implications. It is a huge mistake, one we unfortunately see more often than we'd like.

In the Strategy Laws, we will walk you through how to create a brand storytelling strategy in a way that differentiates your company and lays the foundation for the stories you bring to life.

■■■THE STRATEGIC BLUEPRINT LAW■■■

Consider the following:

1. Strategy
2. Approach
3. Storytelling Framework™

Let's look at each one.

Strategy

Strategy is critical to successful execution. You need a deep understanding of where you've been, were you currently are, and where you want to go. You need to look at the big picture.

When defining your strategy, you first need to look at the key objectives of: (1) the company, (2) your department, and (3) your functional team. Your strategy must support all three.

Effective strategy requires a set of key elements that your executive sponsors would want to see. We demonstrate one below.

Key elements of the brand storytelling strategy:

- Current approach to brand storytelling within the organization
- The vision of how you want the approach to evolve in the next 3, 6, 12, and 18 months

- Proposed strategic approach:
  - Goals and objectives
  - Key priorities
  - Key executing drivers
- Reasons for the proposal, benefits, the why
- Proof points: any insights either an audit or analysis uncovered that support the suggested approach
- A phased plan of enablement and scaling
- Required resources:
  - Executive support
  - People
  - Budget
  - Process changes and cultural shifts necessary
- Supporting infrastructure needed
- Projected outcomes and key performance indicators (KPIs); proposed structure for regular reporting
- Timelines
- Current and potential challenges for achieving success
- Examples of similar programs currently in the industry and beyond
- Decisions that need to be made
- Next steps

We won't dive into each one of these elements. They are self-explanatory. However, we do want to point out that your strategy shouldn't be static. It should adapt to market changes, customer expectations, and the insights you continue to uncover during execution. The big objectives will probably not change as often, but your approach might and execution definitely will. If they do stay static, that is your number one indication that you are doing something wrong.

Approach

Once you are clear on your strategy, outline your approach. If you are a large brand and partner with an agency (or multiple agencies) on creative ideation and execution, you must agree on the approach that will support your strategic direction.

For one of the most interesting approaches to storytelling, let's take a look at Havas, one of the top advertising and public relations agencies.

Havas first caught our eye when it launched the Annex, an agency that lives at the epicenter of youth culture and commerce. Powered by creators instead of traditional agency creatives, the agency has cracked the code on building culturally relevant brands and experiences for Fortune 200 brands as well as emerging labels. The Annex is a physical space where emergent cultural trends and phenomena are captured by people who are actually living them. Through the meaningfully playful interactions that take place within and around each of the Annex spaces, creative, content, and other key business leaders are able to capture the spirit embodied in the codes of culture. Havas describes the Annex as "the voice of emerging culture."

On the front page of Havas's website it says:

CULTURE NEVER SLEEPS

In order to be on the pulse of what's happening, you have to be part of it.

And that's why we started The Annex.

While other agencies just observe and latch onto existing culture, we help create it.

By building a model that welcomes creative minds from more than just advertising backgrounds—artists, photographers, musicians, fashion designers, social media influencers, people who had never even heard industry buzzwords like "millennial" before—we've created a unique environment that puts us at the center of culture as it grows.

That makes every one of our Annex events first-hand market research, giving us an up-close look at how culture constantly evolves—and an authentic perspective on how to approach our clients' creative work.[1]

We wanted to know more. So we sat down with two amazing women and veterans of the industry, Tatia Torrey, president and chief client officer, and Anna Parker, chief strategy officer of Havas, to talk about their approach to brand storytelling. What we found was fascinating!

The team at Havas has built an operational framework for how they develop big ideas, anchored in a deep understanding of how culture impacts the brand and its customers specifically, which ultimately become award-winning advertising and customer engagement frameworks for some of the most notable brands in the United States. By creating a repeatable methodology, the framework acts as an "engine," efficiently churning out unique, innovative, fresh perspectives for its clients (Figure 2.1).

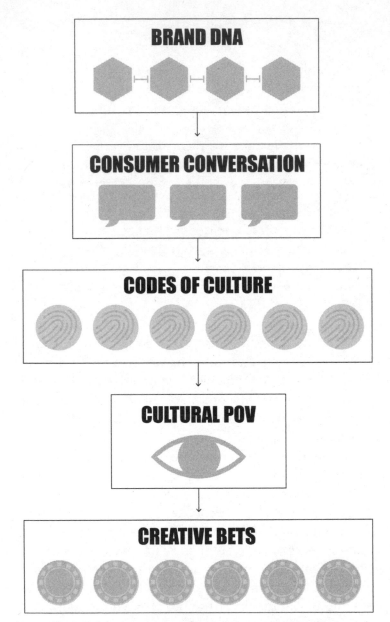

FIGURE 2.1   Havas's framework for developing ideas

The key steps of Havas's approach to storytelling include:

1. **Brand DNA**
   Begin by investigating elements of the brand's DNA, both historical and current, to understand its genetic makeup in terms of how consumers engage with, interact with, and perceive the brand. This can include everything from a brand's origin story and personality, to unique elements of its process or products, to branding elements used over the years: logos, characters, language, sounds.

2. **Consumer Conversation**
   The agency invests deeply in forensic analysis of real-time conversations between and with real people. The goal here is to find out who is talking about the brand, what they're saying, why, and a host of other critical attributes about these people: Are they detractors or advocates? Do they simply consume brand content, or do they share it in their networks? What are their psychographic profiles, and how have those profiles changed as the dynamics of culture have changed around them? As an example, if you want to understand a brand's business challenges, just look at what customers are complaining about on Twitter. If you want to understand a brand's role in people's lives, do an analysis of unpaid reviews, or consider a content analysis of user-generated photos that bring the brand's consumer and cultural context to life. Social data—reviews, posts, comments, photos—is one of the largest and richest datasets at our disposal. You just have to ask the right questions. The

agency uses a variety of tools to understand both qualitative and quantitative insights that reveal consumer behaviors and brand opportunities.

3. **Codes of Culture**
   Armed with findings from research on consumer behaviors, attitudes, and passion points, decide which aspects of culture matter most to the brand: technology, music, language, education, food, and so on. Identify the Codes of Culture, the consumer stories or expressions of these cultural dynamics.

4. **Cultural Point of View (POV)**
   Synthesize learnings on the brand, consumers, and culture into client-specific and Havas-specific artifacts so that both companies' teams internalize what this critical discussion adds to everyone's mutual understanding of brand, prospect, and customer. This Cultural Point of View typically includes one or two key insights that push past the culture you observe. It describes an ideal future state for the type of culture the brand wants to create or wants its customers to be associated with.

5. **Creative Bets**
   With this framework in hand, the team leverages cultural insights and ideates on content that brings those stories and the Cultural POV to life. The agency model is designed to produce many testable and "try-able" ideas, executed by in-house designers and creatives for lower production efficiencies.

Tatia explains, "The need to be relevant requires an always-on mentality as well as the instantaneous response to what's happening in modern culture to make brands feel more alive. Our integrative framework and methodology brings together all the necessary mindsets and talent to be always-on, so that we can help them provide the right messaging at the right time with the right value proposition wherever they are."

She further elaborates: "That's why we have shifted the agency model from art director/writer teams to creator teams dedicated to brands. Once they're immersed in the brand's cultural codes they can create content in real time that's also on strategy. That's where the magic happens."

When we asked how the agency partners with brands beyond the point of content creation, Anna said that "in the most successful instances, it is absolutely a holistic team effort." Their teams are referred to as "hives" and consist of the creator teams, community managers, analysts, and strategists, all working as one in a buzzy newsroom atmosphere, surfacing information that feeds responses, insights, and agile content creation.

Here is the coolest part: when they work with a brand that is truly an evangelist for this approach, this feeds back into the corporate management of the brand because the insights then impact other parts of the business, such as determining what products to launch or what the in-store experience should look like.

Tatia adds, "The lucky thing about culture is that it shapes everything, from what we wear, say, and eat. Understanding what is going on with culture helps shape that 360-degree customer experience. It's all interconnected. For our work on QSR [quick service restaurant] brands, we brought forward things that are going on in the fashion world, and now that is impacting the way uniform design might look for that brand.

Once you tap into the things that are happening in culture that matter to your consumers, you almost can't help but see the way it applies to these other aspects of the brand experience."

An amazing approach for sure. But what does it look like up close and personal as the team partners with a brand on its execution?

In late 2017, CKE Restaurants, the parent company of Carl's Jr. and Hardee's, began a search for a new agency partner to reinvigorate its brand(s) and generate engagement and consideration that converts to restaurant traffic and transactions. Faced with stiff competition, shifting food trends, and marketing that had missed the mark, CKE had to break through the incredibly competitive QSR category.

CKE was dealing with brand relevancy and declining transactions. It was a bifurcated brand in a cluttered and competitive category. It needed to define the brand stories for the Carl's Jr. and Hardee's brands and create messaging that provided resonance, point of difference, consumer engagement, and value perception.

Throughout the pitch process, Havas used its storytelling framework, discovering each brand's cultural codes and using them to inform unique cultural POVs and resulting creative platforms. Recognizing that the two brands had more differences than similarities, Havas leaned into the brand DNA and cultural codes of each brand's unique consumer base.

The Carl's Jr. brand has always had a larger-than-life personality, but culture had evolved faster than the creative. Havas set out to develop a solution that made the food the real object of desire, with irresistible imagery and iconic product descriptors to create Crave Culture (Figure 2.2).

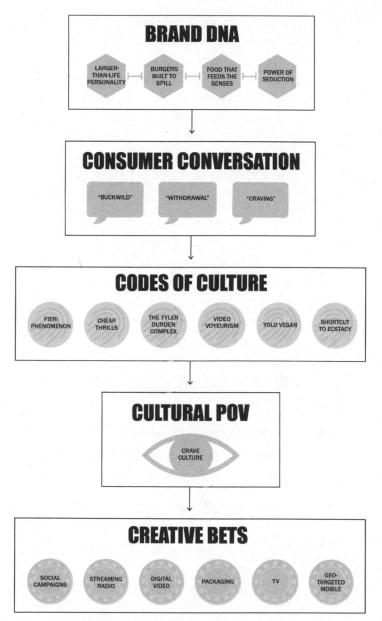

FIGURE 2.2   Havas's solution for Carl's Jr.

Here's the team's storytelling approach to Carl's Jr. in their own words.

Brand DNA: We were inspired by the personality of Carl's Jr.'s founder, the unique way they stack ingredients on their burgers, even their previous advertising. We didn't want to lose the seductive power of their food, but needed to express it in a modern way.

> Larger-Than-Life Personality
> Burgers Built to Spill
> Food That Feeds the Senses
> Power of Seduction

Consumer Conversation: We found many examples of people describing the way they're "tempted" by the food, the power it has over them, and we were inspired by the exciting language they used to describe the food.

"I'm craving it because the hot delicious cheesy flavor is tempting me"

"I need to feed my burger withdrawal"

"What makes it so craveable is the cheese melting off the sides . . . it makes me go buckwild!"

Codes of Culture: We saw evidence of people who were tired of all the advice on *avoiding* cravings. Outta the way, kale! They wanted to get back to burgers.

Fieri Phenomenon	Cheap Thrills	The Tyler Durden Complex
Video Voyeurism	YOLO Vegan	Shortcut to Ecstasy

Cultural POV: We summed this up with two simple words that describe the culture the brand creates:

Crave Culture

Creative Bets. The campaign came to life across all channels through the fast-moving content creation process developed by the Havas team. From Insta Stories and creative image grids to TV commercials and fun T-shirts, we amplified the brand's personality that resonated with its community.

In contrast, the Hardee's brand is rooted in community and a sense of pride in its process. While Carl's Jr.'s Brand DNA is Food that Feeds the Senses, Hardee's is Food that Feeds the Soul. At Hardee's, the lights are on at 4 a.m. as the baker starts making the first batch of biscuits from scratch.

The Cultural Codes Havas uncovered celebrated Cast Iron Culture and Flyover Fashion, emerging trends originating in flyover states and inspiring the East and West Coasts, not the other way around. This all came together in a very different Cultural POV: Comfort Culture. This idea leverages Hardee's credibility in comfort food, propelled by the confidence that comes from being comfortable with who you are. This strategy inspired a creative platform that celebrates the effort that goes into the brand's handmade American classics while contemporizing the look and feel of the American heartland.

The fast-food category is a crowded marketplace, and both of these brands were Davids in the face of the Goliaths of the industry. Getting the brand's story out required an always-on mentality and approach. In addition to the standard limited time offers and promotional campaigns, the brands needed to make noise daily to break through and be top of mind in the moment of that critical daily decision, "What am I going to eat?" Havas's always-on, hived approach provides content creation supporting campaigns and reacting to real-time cultural events.

A great example, no doubt. But the question is: how can you use Havas's approach to create your own?

A great storytelling approach recognizes:

- Where you have been: all the equities built into the brand over time
- Where you are today: insights into consumers' lives and the role the brand or product plays today
- Where you are going: the cultural codes, trends, and tensions that show us where culture is headed and what the brand role could be tomorrow

Here are five simple steps you can take:

1. Outline who you are as a brand: your story, your values, your voice, what you stand for. Use it as an overarching theme. We would even go so far as suggesting building out the timeline of your company's history and mapping out the evolution of your brand's identity. Then:
   a. Identify what differentiates you from the others.
   b. Find the stories long forgotten or those that went unnoticed that show what made your brand identity what it is today.

    c. Search for the defining moments that organically highlight your company's authenticity and its true self.

2. Understand your audience: their preferences, the latest trends they are into, what they say about you and your products, what they like and dislike about competitors' brands and products, what content they like and share the most, and so on. The key here isn't to use your (potentially) outdated consumer personas; rather, gather real-time insights from rich social data, analyzing the latest social media conversations, reviews, and even photos (visual listening allows you to glean insights from images). Remember, in today's fast-paced world, consumer preferences change much more quickly than one expects, so relying on focus groups and annual surveys is no longer the best approach. This might seem complicated, but try doing a quick search on Twitter using a variety of keywords and hashtags around your brand, and you will be surprised what golden nuggets you can uncover. Of course, if you are a large brand, you'll have access to a set of more sophisticated tools to do your data mining and analysis.

3. Create stories that integrate all three:
    a. Your DNA (your core beliefs and values)
    b. Consumers' attitudes and your mutually shared passions
    c. Current cultural dynamics and the latest cultural phenomena

4. Choose the creative approach and relevant formats to tell your stories based on the above considerations.

5. Don't just do it once (for example, for your big product launch), but build out the evergreen content calendar of stories that will continue to engage your communities and consumers at large in your conversations. Remember to try out new things and adapt with the times and consumer preference shifts.

The Storytelling Framework™

Once you put together your strategy and identify your approach, you'll be well equipped to create a storytelling framework for your brand. We have created this framework to help you think through the key questions that usually arise as you move from strategy to execution.

You will have insights from your audit, a solid understanding of the performance of your current content, customer insights (what customers like, frequently asked questions, topics of interest, preferred platforms, and more), cultural shifts that might impact your storytelling strategies, and so on.

Now you need to decide on each of the 13 elements of the storytelling framework (Figure 2.3). These will answer most of the questions that will arise during execution. The rest of the book is designed not only to walk you through all 13 elements but to provide tips, inspire ideas, and even offer words of caution where applicable.

WHO	Brand: voice + personality Consumer: themes + insights
WHY	Goals (based on personas + audience insights)
WHAT	Content mix (types and formats)
WHERE FROM	Sourcing the stories
WHERE	Channel mix
HOW	Content calendar
HOW OFTEN	Frequency
HOW FAST	Agile processes + response playbooks
WITH WHOM	Partnerships: customers, employees, agencies, influencers . . .
HOW FAR	Paid amplification strategy
HOW MUCH	$
HOW EFFECTIVE	Optimization approach
HOW RESPONSIVE	Community engagement plan

FIGURE 2.3   The Storytelling Framework™

To illustrate the storytelling framework in action, let's look at a brand example. Not just any brand, one of our favorites.

NKD Wines is the brainchild of Naked Winery, based in Oregon. On its website, nakedwinery.com, it states:

> Wine drinkers can be choosers. Naked Winery's brands were designed with that in mind. Just like the members of any family, each of our brands has its own personality and story to tell. Find out more about them and see which wines suit you best.

We don't mind if we do.

Naked Winery has several brands:

- NKD Wines: *Live NKD. Be NKD. Drink NKD. For yourself, for the experience, for something entirely different.*
- Outdoor Vino: *Take it outside! Wine bottled in reusable, recyclable, durable BPA-free plastic that's meant to be shared among nature.*
- Oh! Orgasmic Wine Co.: *Tonight's the night for a truly premium wine experience.*
- Naked Cowboy Wines: *Can a cowboy drink wine? Damn straight.* (A partnership with Robert John Burck, the Naked Cowboy who is widely associated with New York City's Times Square and wears only cowboy boots, a hat, and briefs with his guitar strategically placed to give the illusion of nudity.)

If these fun brand names and on-brand partnerships didn't catch your attention, we don't know what will.

Except maybe the company's fun billboards that say: "Naked Winery. We Aim to Tease."

Even though each one of these brands is unique in its own right, for the purposes of our example let's focus on NKD Wines. Why? Because this brand truly stands out in the crowded space.

In a space where there are so many wines to choose from and where brands focus on the wine's terroir and grape varietals, NKD Wines stands out as accessible and exciting. It's ideal for someone who might be overwhelmed by choice sophistication and wants something fun to share with a group of friends. Playful, not stuffy. Social, not snobby. "Craft beer brings people together in a fun way. So why not wine?" thought the founders. What a great way to introduce itself to the market.

Let's look at the brand's guidelines:

Brand Identity

Launched by Naked Winery in July 2016, NKD wines are "fun and youthful. The goal was to create a bold, innovative beverage that authentically connects to a new, youthful audience. . . . Made in the Pacific Northwest with a wide range of white and red varieties, NKD is breaking the mold by focusing on wine as being social, while nourishing relationships with a youthful wild streak. We connect to active Millennial/ Gen Y's and the young at heart."[2]

Brand Tone and Character

Personal, playful, fun, inspiring, and whimsical. The stuffy wine world it's not. Out of the box colors, promotions, social media, and merchandise with personality and vibe and crazy events to match.

Mission

> Live NKD. Be NKD. Drink NKD. For yourself, for
> the experience, for something entirely different.

You can find the "Brand Identity at a Glance" information at nkdwine.com as well (Figure 2.4). And why
not? Why not make it easily available to customers
who are looking to find out more about your products?
It's a great approach!

FIGURE 2.4   NKD's "Brand Identity at a Glance"

The color choices for the logo were intentional. Each wine has a different colored logo: Chardonnay—green; Cabernet Sauvignon—red; Pinot Gris—yellow; Pinot Noir—purple; Red Blend—blue; Rosé—pink (Figure 2.5). The company did plenty of research in not only their market, but the color series as well. The brand is unique in the industry for helping customers move away from saying: "I like Pinot Noir" to: "I like the purple one." You are probably wondering, "Why would the company do that?"

FIGURE 2.5   NKD wine labels

"We wanted to take the intimidation out of wine," Stephanie Prange, marketing maven at Naked Winery, told us. "We wanted to open up the doors to new wine drinkers and make the choice easy for them while being fun and playful."

Furthermore, every single wine has a personality, which is depicted on the bottle's back label. While other wineries are just talking about the flavors of wine, NKD is hoping to invoke adventure and experiences with its wines. We encourage you to go to the website (nkdwine.com) and check it out for yourself. Let's look at Jessica's favorite, Rosé.

Wine: NKD Rosé
What to Expect When Imbibing:
- Uninhibited selfies
- Discover hidden talents
- Impulsive road trips to nowhere

Flavor: Luscious melon aromas and cranberry flavors
Eats: Grilled salmon with lime butter sauce and asparagus

We love this because whereas other wineries' websites highlight their chateaus, their vineyards, and their grapes, NKD's website does the complete opposite.

The brand truly caters to the millennial generation. Millennials are into experiences. As a result, the brand looked at its product as the vehicle to the experience. It was not about pairing the wine with the food; it was about pairing the wine with the experience.

Each summer NKD Wines are served at one of Oregon's largest outdoor concert venues. The Les Schwab Amphitheater in Bend, Oregon, features performers from folk music to rock in an outdoor riverfront amphitheater in the Historic Old Mill District. "We've had such a great time serving our wines at Les Schwab Concerts. It helps us to connect locally and share in a great experience with those who love our wines," says Stephanie.

And because the brand hits the mark, it has a solid following. But here's what's cool. The company doesn't toot its own horn. It lets its ambassadors tell their stories about their experiences with the wine. Brilliant because they know that word of mouth is much more powerful and credible with the millennial crowd than brand promotion. The company turns its super fans into brand ambassadors.

Because it is such a new brand, it hasn't yet invested heavily into paid media. A lot of excitement around NKD Wines has been organic. And ambassadors play a huge role in that. Stephanie explains: "People come to us. They try out our wine, they fall in love with our brand and its vibe, and they ask us how they could get involved. So we let them run with the story. They go on adventures, bring the wine with them, and post lots of pictures sharing their experiences (Figures 2.6a and 2.6b). We then reshare those. And it grows from there. That's how our ambassador program got started."

FIGURE 2.6A   NKD ambassadors tell their own stories

FIGURE 2.6B   NKD ambassadors post
pictures sharing their experiences

As new wines come out, ambassadors tell new stories and promote to their followers. The brand is also very open to feedback and new partnerships. Passion, creativity, and alignment with the brand's mission are key.

The company also does something totally unique, and in our humble opinion, quite delicious: it creates custom wines (and labels, of course) for the major holidays. There was a "Fugly Sweater" Red Blend for Christmas and "Be Mine" Rosé for Valentine's Day.

"The seasonal labels are a lot of fun to do," says Cory Cae Willamson, Naked Winery Art Director. "A while back we were approached by Amazon Wines and asked to create a special Halloween label (Figure 2.7). Which we did. We then followed up by creating the Christmas label (Figure 2.8). Customers loved the wines, and it made for great holiday gifts. We had a ton of social media interactions around both campaigns, and it generated a number of great stories. So we carried it into Valentine's Day, and partnered with our ambassadors on telling their romantic stories with wine (Figure 2.9)."

FIGURE 2.7   NKD Halloween label

FIGURE 2.8   NKD Christmas label

FIGURE 2.9   NKD Valentine's Day label

And then they looked around to see if anyone was doing the same in the industry. The answer was "not really." With craft beer, you hear about seasonal releases all the time (for example, the pumpkin beer for fall). So the company thought: why can't we do the same thing in the wine industry? What a great opportunity for innovation!

And that's another reason we love the NKD brand! It is open to trying new things. Not only is it cool, it's a great distribution selling point. A lot of stores are looking for unique seasonal products to showcase on their shelves. What do people look for during Valentine's Day? Chocolate, flowers, and wine. The product practically sells itself.

The company also has crazy fun merchandise, which it sources from local Oregon companies that Pacific Northwest consumers love. Local partnerships are super important to the brand, and that fact is appreciated by its clients and ambassadors alike. What's our personal favorite? It's hard to choose. After all, there is a Hydro Flask that says, "Let's get naked." But we'll have to go with the calendar (Figure 2.10). Sounds boring, right? Guess again! Here's what the back of the calendar says: "At Naked Winery, we're on a mission to cut America's divorce rate in half by inviting couples to share a glass of wine nightly. We created our calendar with fun Date Night ideas to keep the flames of love burning!" From "write a secret love note and put it in your partner's pocket" to "explore the city while on rollerblades and end the date with ice cream cones," for every day of the year there is a suggestion on how to spice up the time with your loved one (Figure 2.11).

FIGURE 2.10   Naked Winery calendar

						Matchmaker Club Month
Sunday	*Monday*	*Tuesday*	*Wednesday*	*Thursday*	*Friday*	*Saturday*
28	29	30	31	1 Make a date to have a date! Plan a mystery date for each other to do this month.	2 **Groundhog Day** PDX SEAFOOD & WINE FEB 2-3 —> Whether there's a shadow or not, there's a 100% chance of wine!	3 SOUTH DAKOTA SPECIAL NAKED EVENT ROARING 20s PARTY in BEND Show and tell day... use your imagination!
4 **Super Bowl** Invite the friends over and cheer on your team! Don't forget the wines!	5 Start the week off steamy! Leave a naughty note on the mirror for them to see when they get out of the shower.	6 Obsessed with Dancing with the Stars? It's time to test your own skills by taking a couple's dance class.	7 **National Rose Day** PNW SPORTSMEN'S SHOW FEB 7-11 —> Surprise your sweetie with a single rose and multiple kisses.	8 Order take out and spend the evening in. Watch a foreign film without subtitles and guess what's happening!	9 Starry night! Find a planetarium and watch the night sky light up.	10 Go sledding! Build a snow fort. Finish the day with a thermos of cocoa with a kick!
11 **Man Day** Mystery date night...HIS choice!	12 How you start the day matters! Spend the morning giving your partner a little extra sweetness.	13 **Mardi Gras** Reminisce about your first date over chocolate and a bottle of Committed. What drew you to each other?	14 **Valentine's Day** Write love letters for the future and tuck them away until next year.	15 Give each other a sincere compliment today. How has your partner improved themselves?	16 **COUPLES RETREAT** in LEAVENWORTH FEB 16th to 19th Make her breakfast in bed.	17 SOUTH DAKOTA NAKED COMEDY NIGHT Go out for late night dessert.
18 **National Drink Wine Day!** OREGON COAST WOMEN'S SHOW Pop open your favorite Naked bottle and celebrate!	19 **President's Day** Who or what inspires you to achieve more? Why? Discuss with your partner.	20 **National Love Your Pet Day** TAKE IT OUTSIDE! Take your pup out to play in the snow at a dog friendly park.	21 Happy Hump Day! Meet each other for lunch and share details of your day.	22 NEWPORT SEAFOOD & WINE FEST FEB 22-25 —> PDX SPRING HOME & GARDEN SHOW FEB 22-25 —>	23 PDX GOLF SHOW FEB 23-25 —> Heat things up with a hot stone couple's massage.	24 Visit a nursing home and spend time listening to their stories. They may even have some great love advice!
25 Pick a music station and have a lazy morning making pancakes together.	26 Indulge in decadence! Treat your sweet tooth with rich chocolate cake and a bottle of Dominatrix.	27 Draw up a warm bubble bath and cozy up to each other. Don't forget the chilled bottle of Frisky Sparkling!	28 Create some wine cocktails! Don't feel like venturing out in the cold for a drink? Bring the bar to you!	1	2	3 National Mulled Wine Day National Unplugging Day

FIGURE 2.11   Calendar page with ideas to keep the flame burning

But what truly drives the wine's success is the company's culture. "We are living what we are selling," says Cory Cae. "We are out there, experiencing life, connecting with people, having fun. Our former employees turn into our ambassadors because they want to stay connected with the company and the product."

Cory Cae also does a lot of product glamor shots for the company. She has a degree in photography. It's her passion. And it shows. From beach scenes to nighttime fun, the content boasts a variety of fun stories. A lot of lifestyle shots come from ambassadors as well. But employees participate in content ideation and creation, too. They are all outgoing, fun personalities that work well together. Some love puns; some are phenomenal kayakers and rock climbers; some love music. And everyone contributes to the content calendar.

Naked Winery doesn't just promote the culture of inclusion, but innovation as well. "NKD Wines specifically is a great opportunity for us to not just follow the trends, but set the trends in the industry," says Corina Farrar, Naked Winery's chief operating officer. "NKD is a really fun brand to experiment with and do things that no one else is doing because that naturally falls within the spirit of the brand."

Well said!

If we plug NKD Wines' brand strategy and approach into the storytelling framework we showed you earlier in the chapter, the table shows what it would look like at a high level.

NKD Wines Storytelling Framework	
WHO	Based on the industry and consumer insights, NKD Wines leadership understood that there isn't a fun, approachable brand that appeals to a younger audience in the market. NKD is breaking the mold by focusing on wine as being social, while nourishing relationships with a youthful wild streak.
WHY	The ultimate goal is to put NKD wines into everyone's hands. However, because the brand is new, NKD focused on awareness first. By creating fun content, offering unique social events, and creating an ambassador program, the brand stands out in the crowded market. Key metrics: engagement, word of mouth, sales.
WHAT	NKD's team utilizes a good mix of content with visuals, images, and video being primary formats. However, it is not about the brand's agenda; it is about consumers' agendas, focusing on highlighting not the product but the stories its ambassadors, customers, and employees are creating.
WHERE	The primary channel of engagement with customers is Instagram. That's where the brand's ambassadors and fans are most active. Secondary channels: Facebook, Twitter, website, forums, search, billboard ads.
WHERE FROM	NKD sources stories from ambassadors, employees, and customers. They also do a good job of cocreating and telling the stories with their local partners who are prominent in the community.

NKD Wines Storytelling Framework	
HOW	The team has a content calendar that is 50 percent fixed (focusing on the known holidays and seasonal announcements: rosés and whites during warmer seasons, reds in the fall and winter) and 50 percent fluid (taking advantage of real-time storytelling opportunities).
HOW OFTEN	The team doesn't have a set frequency. They target quality over quantity, but create and post content often enough to stay top of mind.
HOW FAST	The team is responsive across content creation and customer engagement. They are agile in responding to market and idea opportunities.
WITH WHOM	The NKD brand is open to partnerships across the board: celebrities, ambassadors, suppliers, employees, customers, etc. They don't outsource their content creation, but do all of it in-house.
HOW FAR	Because Naked Winery focuses on the distribution model, paid amplification is invested in content discovery around new members and partners.
HOW MUCH	Always-on flexible budget.
HOW EFFECTIVE	The team optimizes based on location, age, and seasonality, and across channels for both organic and paid media.
HOW RESPONSIVE	The team's policy is "no comment goes unanswered" (through all channels: social, website, public forums, etc.). They also reach out to brand lovers and build relationships with them, bringing a select few into the ambassador program.

What we love about the Naked Winery team is that to them *possibilities* is not a noun, but a verb. They don't focus on what was, but on what can be and what's to come. And we applaud them for that.

THE COLLABORATION LAW

Take note: your strategy won't be successful if you create and execute it in a bubble. Silos are the number one killer of even the most well-thought-out approaches. Silos produce not only dangerous brand inconsistencies but cost redundancies and overall inefficiency across teams, initiatives, and campaigns.

For your storytelling framework to work effectively, you have to consider both macro and micro stories. The latter are being created every single day at different customer touchpoints by employees across functions (branding, PR, marketing, customer care, sales, HR, etc.) and geographies. Every story contributes to the overall perception of your brand, your culture, and your products.

Today, considering the stories you create across your company isn't enough. You have to consider the overall immersive experience your customer has with your organization and the stories consumers will share based on those experiences. Aligning all of those functions around your strategy, approach, and framework is more critical than ever. That is the reason customer experience management (CXM) has become the central focus for most leadership teams over the past several years. Chief experience officer has emerged as a new role that sometimes replaces the chief marketing officer function in some organizations.

Creating a solid strategy isn't enough anymore. You have to put processes in place to align the organization around that strategy and hire—or outsource—the right skill sets to maximize the impact of its execution. We will discuss this in more detail in Chapter 4 when we introduce the 6 Ps of Real-Time Marketing.™ But before we look at that, let's talk about finding your story.

Chapter 3

THE DISCOVERY LAWS

FIND YOUR STORY

One of the most frequent questions we get when we engage with companies large and small is, "Where do we find the stories?"

It doesn't matter how big you are, what industry you are in, and what your product is—every single brand is struggling with finding authentic stories that will resonate. And no wonder. They are often constrained, forced to promote a product instead of looking beyond the features and functions, beyond the next marketing campaign.

Great stories are different from traditional brand messages. They don't include product benefits and pricing offers. They are beautifully messy. They hold us spellbound and make us think. Great stories don't simply appear. They are discovered along the way. Storytelling is a creative journey, not a short-term product launch.

Before we take a deeper look at the discovery laws, however, let's consider the key misconceptions that often get in the way of our creative journey.

Misconception #1

"If our story is not remarkable, it's not worth telling." This is absolute BS! First off, "remarkable" is in the eye of the beholder. Second, your story doesn't have to go viral to be impactful. Besides being dramatic, unbelievable, or hilarious, your story could do so many things: inspire people to make a small step toward their dream, educate them on the right approach to creating something, telling them they are not alone, the list is looooong. There are many ways to relate; the sky's the limit.

Misconception #2

"Our stories should make everyone happy." Your storytelling goal shouldn't be to make everyone happy. You are not ice cream! Unless you are in the business of amusing, entertaining, or making every single person on the planet happy (such as Disney or Baskin-Robbins). What you need to focus on is your target audience (no matter how small), people who "get" you. It'll grow from there, trust us. Stay true to your authentic self and to your community, and you will not fail.

Misconception #3

"Our product is boring. No story will make it attractive." For every boring product, there is a community that uses it and appreciates it. If Charmin can make toilet paper interesting through storytelling, you can do the same. Just look at Maersk, the Danish transport and logistics conglomerate. Its Instagram page boasts over 100,000 followers, and it's a page dedicated to pictures and videos of shipping vessels and shipping containers. Shipping containers! Strangely enough, its community is highly engaged. And not only on Instagram. It has millions of fans on its Facebook page, several very active LinkedIn groups that debate industry trends, and a number of other social media channels through which it connects with its niche audiences.

These misconceptions—or shall we say excuses?—prevent you from thinking big, from unearthing the most creative ideas and most fascinating stories. Let's take a look at how and where you can find inspiration for your storytelling approach.

THE HERO LAW

Earlier in the book we introduced the concept of macro and micro stories.

Macro stories are at the core of your organization's DNA. They highlight your company's story, its founding myth. Macro stories are the why, the foundation of and the reason for everything the company does.

Micro stories, however, are the lifeblood of your storytelling strategy. They are an always-on approach to continue building on your macro story. They are the moments in time that allow you to keep your brand at the forefront of everyone's mind in a relevant way.

The hero of a macro story is usually the founder of the company. However, the heroes of micro stories vary vastly. Why? Because once a company is created, there are a lot of people who make it work, make it tick, make it successful.

So our advice is to look beyond your macro story and the features and functions of your products and consider the broader ecosystem around you. Carly Simon said it best: "You're so vain, you probably think this song is about you." Well, this song is not about you. Consumers do not want to hear how awesome you are; they want stories they can relate to. And those usually come from putting other people at the center of the story. For example, by making consumers the heroes of the story, you show how you help facilitate their dreams and thus become their trusted ally.

Potential heroes of your stories might be your:

- Customers and their families
- Employees
- Partners
- Franchisees/licensees
- Stakeholders
- Industry peers
- Influencers
- Volunteers
- Mascots
- Causes
- Change movements

Plum Organics, a company that makes health food and snacks for babies and kids, decided to make parents the heroes.

The company launched a campaign provocatively named "Do Your Part[ner]." Yes, you read that right. They invited their customers to make love a priority, encouraging parents everywhere not to lose sight of their own relationships with each other.

This isn't the only interesting conversation Plum has started with parents around the world.

Its #ParentingUnfiltered conversation is quite popular among not only Plum Organics's customers
but parents everywhere. Check it out here: http://
parentingunfiltered.com.

We reached out to Plum's team and got a chance
to sit down with Katie Sobel, VP brand engagement
and marketing communications, and Victoria Fiore,
now former director of brand strategy and mission, to
talk about their approach to storytelling and customer
engagement. Both Katie and Victoria joined the company when it employed fewer than 50 people, and they
have seen it grow and mature. Interestingly, both have
quite diverse backgrounds: Katie has culinary training, and Victoria's interests lie at the intersection of
business and social impact. Plum seems to be a culture
of hybrid thinkers.

Here is what we learned.

First, Plum Organics's stories always tie back
to the company's mission. Plum was founded by
a team of real parents dealing with real parenting
challenges. Most of them aspired to make their own
fresh, homemade, organic baby food. The company's
products—nutritious, organic baby food and kids'
snacks—are designed to make life for parents a bit easier, sans the guilt.

"Whether it's product development or messaging,
it's our belief that it all starts with an intimate knowledge of and camaraderie with our consumer, as a
parent and a person," says Katie.

From its amazing manifesto (http://parenting
unfiltered.com/manifesto) to every single one of its
campaigns, the company is not shy to admit that pres-
sure for parenting perfection doesn't end with baby
food (Figure 3.1).

FIGURE 3.1   Plum Organics manifesto

Second, the company stays true to who it is consistently.

"Even from our scrappy early days before we did any paid advertising, our marketing strategy has consistently shared parent-to-parent content, and engaged in a two-way conversation with our consumers that addresses the real issues parents face and tells them they're not alone, and they're doing a great job muddling through," says Victoria Fiore. "When we got big enough that we could do our first real brand campaign, we decided to more explicitly address this tension between aspiration and reality that was leaving us all feeling like we were constantly falling short. How do we normalize them and start a genuine conversation while maintaining our brand's bright, spunky, playful personality? We launched Parenting Unfiltered and found the conversations it created were not only fun and engaging, but cathartic to the millions of parents in our community." It surpassed their wildest expectations and completely outperformed its spend, earning industry awards and praise from parents (Figure 3.2).

FIGURE 3.2   Tweet by @crazycanonmom

The Do Your Part(ner) campaign is an extension of that same concept, taking a taboo, but entirely real and incredibly important subject and bringing humor and levity to it on a public stage by using the brand as a platform.

The cool part was: the company used data to understand which stories would resonate. The team noticed that the content touching on relationships between parents on Parenting Unfiltered was consistently their highest performing, particularly in terms of engagement.

Victoria Fiore elaborates: "For our Mother's and Father's Day video series, for example, we saw thousands of our parents tagging their partners to share content like 'Dear Mom Who Maybe Never Wants to Have Sex Again' and 'Dear Dad Who Isn't Sure Where to Look During Labor.' The best thing about these public partnership shares was that we were creating moments of connection, however brief or superficial, between two overwhelmed parents. We wanted to create more of that. We've been joking about a Make More Babies campaign for years, and so what was a joke suddenly became a real idea—and an awkwardly hilarious process of choosing an agency partner."

The Do Your Part(ner) campaign wasn't a coincidence. Plum Organics conducted research to see if parents are putting themselves first every once in a while, and here is what they found:

- 70 percent of millennial parents feel guilty when they're away from their child for a night out with their partner
- Nearly 70 percent of parents with a significant other talk about their kids the majority of the time they're alone together

- Over one-third of parents say the thing they do most in their bed besides sleeping is catching up on news or social media
- Parents say they are 52 percent less likely to celebrate Valentine's Day after they become a parent

Interesting stats, especially if you consider that 88 percent of parents think having a good sex life is essential to their family's happiness. So the company decided to address the issue head-on.

And quite successfully so! Just two and a half weeks into the campaign, the main video was seen over 11.4 million times across channels, and the brand received some great industry recognition. But the internal teams were way more excited by the comments they were seeing from parents such as "this is so us" or "we can so relate."

On their website, they provided valuable tips on easy ways to connect with your partners, appropriately called "G-Rated Quickies" (Figure 3.3). Whether you have 30 seconds, 15 minutes, or 3 hours, you will find a lot of ideas you can implement immediately in your own relationship, such as a suggestion to make your better half a playlist for their commute.

FIGURE 3.3   Plum's G-Rated Quickies

Another thing we absolutely love about Plum's approach is the fact that it doesn't ignore its own employees. So many of the actual storylines come from personal experiences within Plum Organics's extended team.

"That's how we get our best ideas," said Victoria. "After that, it's fun to see how many people—from internal leaders to copywriters, production directors, even our legal team—see the content and say, 'Whoa—this is so true.' These exchanges often lead to more personal anecdotes that you don't normally get in professional settings, some of which even make it into the next round of content."

"As a brand by parents for parents, the humanization of our brand has been a huge part of our success," adds Katie. "Sharing personal experiences is how we've learned so much about our consumers, and I believe it's also how they've learned so much about us. We're always showcasing the stories of real parents on our team as part of our external marketing and strategy."

Plum Organics has also invested heavily in building relationships with the influential moms and dads who have their own platforms and communities, where they share their own genuine stories and experiences. Working with these influencers gave them permission to explore the deeper, more reflective side of parenting topics in an authentic way. And it provided a means for the company's stories to extend into the communities that matter to their brand.

"We also created a fun Do Your Part(ner) Kit (Figures 3.4 and 3.5) that's inspired by a date night in, featuring a curated selection of products from some of our favorite brands, from chocolate to massage oil (and, of course, Plum snacks)," said Katie. "We gave

away the kits through our influencers and on Plum's
social channels."

FIGURE 3.4   Plum's Do Your Part(ner) Kit

FIGURE 3.5   Kit insert

The "Do Your Part(ner)" campaign is ultimately an extension of Parenting Unfiltered and a playful way of engaging an even larger audience in brand conversations.

The brand is extending its stories beyond digital. Team members have produced targeted influencer and media events. They have also created fun, tangible engagement pieces with their curated Parenting Survival Kits, which have become wildly popular with their fans. Their brand ambassador program, Plum Parents, is another area through which they were able to extend their #TeamParent message into broader communities with grassroots activities and meetups. The team is also looking to expand their lifestyle campaigns to more experiential stunts and activations in the future.

Putting others at the center of your story pays off every single time.

But what about the times when the brand is not the one controlling the narrative?

There are plenty of those instances. From the tales of amazing culture to the horror stories of unacceptable customer service, a big chunk of stories online are not ones produced by the brand's marketing team, but rather by everyone else. As people experience your product or your service, they talk about every aspect of that interaction with the company, good or bad.

Telling amazing stories isn't enough anymore. You have to create the experience worth talking about. You have to consider the attitude of your employees and the behavior of your executives. You have to ask yourselves: "Are we walking the talk? Are we living what we preach?"

A great example of an executive who truly represented the company and its values was Herb Kelleher, cofounder and former CEO of Southwest Airlines. The stories of his humble leadership and laser focus on customer satisfaction are legendary.

I (Ekaterina) recently keynoted a large event where I presented on the topic of leadership and innovation. My talk prompted a lot of follow-up conversations with attendees. But one story, told to me by Gregg Gregory, the founder of Teams Rock, was especially fascinating.

About 75 years ago Gregory was boarding a Southwest flight out of Orlando, Florida. Way in front of him in the boarding line he noticed a man wearing a giant Mickey Mouse baseball hat. He didn't think anything about it until he walked onto the plane and saw that the gentleman had taken a seat all the way in the back of the plane.

If you have ever flown Southwest, you know it doesn't have assigned seating. People at the front of the line get their pick of the best seats on the plane. And normally they choose the ones up front, either a window or an aisle seat. Not only did this gentleman pick the last row of the airplane, he chose to sit in the middle seat. This struck Gregory as strange. After all, the gentleman was one of the first to board.

As the plane got airborne, Gregory noticed that this man walked all the way up to the front, talked to the flight attendants for a while, and then turned around, walked down the aisle, and started assisting the flight attendants in serving everyone peanuts and drinks. Eventually he came to Gregory's seat and said, "Hi. My name is Herb Kelleher. Thank you for flying my airline. Can I get you something to drink?"

"That to me was a definition of humble leadership and putting customers first," Gregg said. He never forgot it. He is a huge fan of the airline, and he shares that story with all of his business clients. Talk about the power of word of mouth! Herb Kelleher's behavior (which, by the way, aligned with the company's values) and his appreciation of his customers created a rich environment for stories and positive memories for those around him.

Now compare that with the negative coverage of United Airlines: passengers being forcefully dragged off overbooked planes, upgrades being revoked so that the company CEO and his family could travel in comfort, the list goes on. These stories don't instill confidence in the brand, do they?

■ THE ACTIONABLE INTELLIGENCE LAW ■

Jeff Bezos, founder and CEO of Amazon, famously said, "Your brand is what other people say about you when you're not in the room."[1] The prevalence of digital and social media means that every day, a never-ending stream of conversations, reviews, and opinions shared online shapes a powerful narrative about your company. From the content they research, to the conversations they have and visuals they share, you can use the real-time insights to uncover key themes and topics that inspire incredible stories.

Social Media Is a 24/7 Real-Time Focus Group

Whether you're launching a new campaign or seeking validation for the types of stories to bring to market, digital and social media can bring actionable insights to the table. Whether you leverage them as a focus group to test new ideas or mine them for insights, the 24/7 nature of these channels makes them a valuable resource.

RadioShack learned this lesson the hard way in 2009 when it attempted to rebrand itself as "The Shack." The goal was to breathe new life into the brand and build trust with younger customers during a time of incredible competition when numerous electronics stores were going out of business.

The company asserted that "The Shack" was a long-time nickname from customers and investors. Except, when customers and the news media heard about this "nickname," they didn't quite agree with that statement.

Twitter exploded with unflattering feedback, and tech media pundits had a field day digging into RadioShack's name change. Wired.com wrote, "It's almost embarrassing, like seeing your grandfather listening to an iPod and riding a single speed track bike. Wait, that actually would be cool."[2]

Engadget.com said, "We're not sure 'The Shack' is the right direction . . . unless they wanted us to immediately picture a remote location where very, very bad things happen."[3]

Technologizer.com hit the nail on the head, commenting, "If the signage outside the store changes but the experience inside doesn't, it's not going to be any more competitive than it is right now."[4]

In response to the feedback, RadioShack kept its name.

Lee Applbaum, chief marketing officer of RadioShack at the time of the campaign, concluded, "When you contemporize an iconic brand, when you in any way seek to change that, it makes people uncomfortable, and I understand that. I think [the criticism] is a reflection on the passion people have for an iconic brand. If people aren't uncomfortable, then you haven't done your job in being transformative."[5]

While Lee is correct that massive brand changes can and will make some customers uncomfortable, the bigger issue here is that in rewriting the brand's story, RadioShack lost its sense of purpose. It was struggling to remain relevant amid a challenging business climate, and a cosmetic makeover was not enough to solve the problems under the hood.

The silver lining with any epic fail is how you learn and adapt from your mistakes.

As you discover your story, it's easy to geek out or get painfully invested in defining and mapping out who you are as a brand. But if you only look inward and focus on yourself, you're missing the big picture. Companies need to factor in how customers perceive their brand, their products and services, and those of their key competitors.

Not only can insights reduce risk, they can inform better brand positioning and more relevant story angles or uncover new trends or customer needs.

Consider Every Customer Touchpoint and Interaction a Powerful Opportunity

With social media, there have never been more opportunities to easily capture insights in real time, but companies shouldn't limit themselves to those channels. Every customer touchpoint and interaction provides a powerful opportunity to capture feedback to understand likes, loves, wishes, and pain points.

Start by asking:

- What channels do our customers spend time on?
- Where do they provide feedback or make requests?
- What are the frequently asked questions about our company versus our competitors?

- Is the overall sentiment positive, negative, or neutral?
- What are the top likes, dislikes, and requests about our company versus our competitors?
- What are the top performing pages on our website?
- What google search terms bring in the most traffic to our site?
- Who are the top influencers and most passionate customers who reach out or talk about our company regularly?

When I (Jessica) led the social media program for Dunkin' Donuts, I was inspired by how the company viewed its customers as its most powerful asset. So much so that its mantra for its social media program became, "We don't own our channels—our fans do." Every element of the company, from its branding, to the in-store experience, products offered, and stories and content shared, all layered back into Dunkin's purpose of keeping its busy, on-the-go customers running.

Luckily for Dunkin', the feeling was mutual. Dunkin' Donuts's customers were (and still are!) passionate about providing the company with feedback on what they love about the brand and how it can better serve them. Whether it was to the customer service team, via the telephone survey posted at the bottom of every receipt, directly to the franchise owners and store employees, or through social media, the brand had no shortage of customer touchpoints to leverage.

During my time there, I regularly saw the company take top feedback and requests and translate them into new products, services, and even new restaurant locations.

On April 2, 2013, Darren Rovell, a well-known sports journalist with a love for Dunkin', received an image from one of his followers of a glazed donut breakfast sandwich being tested in a few stores in Massachusetts.

Darren took the image and tweeted, "Dunkin' Donuts unveils fried egg sandwich with bacon on donut buns," to his millions of followers.[6]

His followers went crazy for the news. And the vast majority of the comments were positive, such as, "Is it wrong that I was oddly excited about this. Clearly, I've lived in Boston way way way too long," to, "I have to try this," or "I just saw this . . . is this real or an April fools joke?"

Within one hour, Dunkin' had received a call from the Associated Press inquiring about the Glazed Donut Breakfast Sandwich. The inquiry opened the floodgates, both with the news media and with customers online. Naturally, there were some negative comments, but in analyzing feedback across customer touchpoints, it was overwhelmingly curious and positive.

That's when the company's public relations team had a brilliant idea. The Glazed Donut Breakfast Sandwich was made up of existing products already available in Dunkin' Donuts locations nationwide: a fried egg, bacon, and a glazed donut. Could the company fast-track this product to market and make it available in June, just in time for one of its most important days of the year, National Donut Day?

You better believe that the rock star team at Dunkin' made it happen! The effort was truly cross-functional, and customers were thrilled. Many shared their images and feedback on the Glazed Donut Breakfast Sandwich, and the effort reinforced Dunkin's passion and commitment to keeping its customers running.

Make Customer Insights *the Story*

While Dunkin' harnesses the power of customer insights to tell its story and launch new products and services, customer feedback can also become the story.

When I (Jessica) worked for TripAdvisor, the company created a customer survey panel, made up of highly engaged members who were passionate about travel. The goal was to issue surveys on a regular cadence to capture feedback on the business, seek their opinions on bespoke travel topics of interest to inform new trends, and discover the likes and dislikes of travelers.

The company used these and site data, such as unusual spikes in traffic to new destinations or hotels and keyword spikes for words like "bed bugs," to inspire stories, reports, blog posts, and social media content that would be interesting to its customers.

For example, in the 2009 beach and pool etiquette survey that I worked on, TripAdvisor uncovered that 82 percent of travelers thought that people often violated some form of beach or pool etiquette. Their top pet peeve? Hogging beach chairs. There was a trend of people "saving" beachside or poolside chairs by getting up early and leaving their stuff on the chairs for hours, while they were off elsewhere.

As one TripAdvisor Destination Expert commented, "My bugbear is when people throw a towel over one of the highly sought-after sun lounges/cabanas, and then go AWOL."[7]

Identifying this trend allowed TripAdvisor to bring this traveler pain point to life through a mix of public relations, content marketing, and social media storytelling. With data and personalized stories from its Destination Expert member community, the company secured significant press coverage by sparking a conversation and debate on the subject, further supporting the company's purpose of giving travelers a voice and platform to share their opinions and experiences.

Tap Insights to Change the Story—and People's Behavior

An inspiring example of leveraging insights to change your story comes from Sport England. Sport England's research uncovered a persistent gender gap in sports participation in the United Kingdom. It found that nearly 2 million more men than women took part in at least 30 minutes of moderate activity once a week.

At the time, Sport England was actively investing in a number of campaigns and tactics aimed at reducing this gender gap, from health and wellness marketing, to leveraging the London 2012 Olympics as inspiration to get more women into sports and fitness. It also funded projects that gave more women access to childcare, women-only fitness programs, and women's sports leagues to address some of the top barriers to entry uncovered in its research.

While these efforts were successful in increasing overall participation levels for both men and women, the gender gap remained the same. With survey results indicating that 75 percent of women wanted to play more sports, Sport England had to dig deeper to uncover what was stopping them.

It uncovered that for many women, the barrier to entry wasn't always tactical, but emotional: many women were paralyzed by a fear of judgment. Some felt that they were "too fat to get fit," or would "slow everyone down."

Sport England realized that in traditional sports marketing, there was no voice out there for the average woman who likes fitness or sports, but isn't necessarily the expert, let alone looking like one. Most sports marketing ads feature perfectly chiseled fitness models or professional athletes. Where were the women who jiggle a bit when they run? The women who could shake it off or laugh if they missed the goal or lost the game? Or the women who don't have perfect rhythm in that Zumba class, but still rock the moves like they're Beyoncé?

Instead of focusing on fears, Sport England set out to change behavior and perceptions by celebrating what women can do. It launched the This Girl Can campaign, featuring fierce and funny stories from women and girls who had overcome barriers to become more active—on their own terms.

A sassy video set to Missy Elliott's "Get Ur Freak On" opened with a woman adjusting her bikini wedgie before jumping into the pool and proceeded to feature women boxing, playing football, in group fitness classes, and more. All of the women and girls in the video were street-cast across the United Kingdom. They were discovered and filmed for the campaign doing their normal fitness activities.[8]

Other elements of the campaign featured women in sports or fitness classes. One showed a woman biking up a hill on a very gloomy day with the caption, "Still slow. Still lapping everyone on the couch." Another had two girls sparring in karate with the caption, "This is how I get my teenage kicks.[9]"

As Kate Dale, strategic lead: brand and digital at Sport England, said, "Authenticity was absolutely key. I'm sure some of them thought the shoot was going to be glamorous, but we worked them hard. Every drop of sweat you see is genuine. Every red face was hard-earned."[10]

To say that the campaign was a massive success is putting it mildly. This Girl Can sparked a movement. It got 2.8 million women between the ages of 14 and 40 exercising, 1.6 million of whom got back into fitness or tried new activities as a result of its refreshing honesty. The This Girl Can films have been watched over 37 million times on YouTube and Facebook, and the #ThisGirlCan hashtag continues to unite and inspire women.

THE BEYOND-THE-OBVIOUS LAW

While insights are powerful when sourcing ideas for your stories, don't stop at the conversations, topics, and themes. By getting to know the people behind the conversations and their psychographic profiles, which consist of personality traits, values, interests, attitudes, and lifestyles, you can stretch your brand storytelling efforts beyond the obvious.

Consider exploring the following approaches.

Open Your Kimono

People love to know what's going on behind the scenes. Lift the curtain on your corporate life and let your community in. Show them the wonders and struggles that make up your brand, your culture.

In 2013, when I (Ekaterina) was spearheading digital transformation across Intel's business, I remember the day my team tried something new. They snapped an iPhone photo of the engineer's desk and posted it on Facebook with the simple caption "Inside Intel." Nothing else. To anyone outside of their community that photo probably looked rather unremarkable, just a messy desk with hardware parts and a bunch of wires. To Intel's community, however, it was a glimpse of Intel's human side, a celebration of nerds everywhere, something that every fan could relate to. The post ended up being the most liked and commented on that year. It was a revelation back then. But even though it happened what seems like eons ago, even to this day not a lot of brands dare to open their kimono and let their customers in. Those that do it well see amazing responses from their fans.

Celebrate Key Occasions Beyond the Obvious

Celebrating holidays is a given for a lot of brands. New Year's, Valentine's Day, Thanksgiving, the company's key milestones, and many other occasions have all become an opportunity to produce deeply emotional messaging. But this space of seasonal greetings is a bit overcrowded.

Identify unique, nonstandard holidays that your communities would relate to. Websites such as http://holidayinsights.com are a good source of information on some of the most interesting and bizarre days celebrated around the world. Find the ones that will work for your audience and have fun creating content around them. For example, the employees of one of the start-ups I (Ekaterina) advise enjoy riding bikes to work. So it celebrated "bring your bike to work day" by posting pictures of its staff and their bikes and sharing their funniest bike stories.

Wouldn't it be fun to celebrate a Wife Appreciation Day in September or celebrate a Fortune Cookie Day by sending your customers fortune cookies with uplifting messages and fun quotes? Or honor Talk Like a Pirate Day, just like Dunkin' Donuts did.

The company hosted a special Twitter sweepstakes in honor of Talk Like a Pirate Day. Between 9 a.m. and 5 p.m. the followers of @DunkinDonuts on Twitter were asked to tweet at the company Dunkin' Donuts menu items in pirate speak using the official hashtag, #PirateDDay, for a chance to win a "treasARR chest" filled with brand goodies. Folks really got into the spirit of the celebration:

> @BrandyBollman: @DunkinDonuts Ahoy, me Hearties! Aye, This Old Salt would Walk the plank for me Booty, Pumpkin Donut & Pumpkin Coffee Coolatta. #PirateDDay
>
> @alexandrah_rae: A laarrrrge iced coffee with toasted arrrglmond syrup. Oh, and a jelly Munchkin for my parrot!! @DunkinDonuts #PirateDDay
>
> @EricBfromCLE: Ahoy @DunkinDonuts no scurvy here if you shiver me timbers with an apple ciderrr & blueberry cake donut #PirateDDay
>
> @meggyw115: @DunkinDonuts Iced (to shiver me timbers) Caaaarrrrramel Latte matey, with skim milk cause I'm watchin me booty. #PirateDDay

Beyond the fun holidays, company milestone celebrations also give you the opportunity to reflect and share the story of your journey, as well as thank your customers for taking the journey with you.

Don't Sell; Add Value

Instead of pushing your product or service, provide utility to your customers through how-to videos and instructional training. How-to videos are one of the most searched formats online. With the Makers Movement on the rise, people prefer to learn how to do things themselves.

HubSpot, a B2B inbound marketing software company, is known for its amazing content hub. As a matter of fact, to a lot of us HubSpot is synonymous with value-add. From trends to workbooks, from tips to templates, HubSpot's blog provides some of the best resources any marketer may need.

In the B2C space look no further than Unilever's All Things Hair campaign. The brand knew that there were around one billion Google searches relating to hair care monthly; however, hair care videos make up only 15 percent of YouTube's beauty content, most of them from vloggers. Unilever, whose hair care brands include Dove, Suave, TRESemmé, and CLEAR, took advantage of the opportunity. For the first time the company brought all of its hair care brands together to create All Things Hair, the YouTube channel of hair styling tutorial videos from the world's most-followed beauty vloggers, using Unilever products. The channel has become a credible source of information and inspiration on the topic and amassed many millions of views across the globe.[11]

Let Your Employees Have a Say

Your employees are the biggest ambassadors of your culture. Let them tell their stories. You probably have amazing storytellers among your peers, and you don't even know it. Usually it's because executives are afraid that the stories may be less than flattering. It's a shame, really.

Zappos has one of the most admired cultures out there, and it lets every single one of its employees (from janitors to executives) tell their stories to large audiences at events or private gatherings. In fact, Zappos encourages it. The company does very little marketing because its employees and its customers evangelize on its behalf.

Or consider another example. I (Ekaterina) worked with an energy company that started allowing its crews to tell stories of the important work they do to restore power to neighborhoods after a storm or other weather-related disturbance. Paired with timely updates, this approach significantly reduced complaints from consumers. Watching the videos of the company employees working hard for their customers, people were able to put themselves in the shoes of company employees and appreciate their efforts.

Educate and Inspire

Don't assume that just because you know something basic or simple, it's common knowledge. Sometimes what's simple to us is novel to others. Share your expertise as much as you can, bring your customers and industry peers into discussions on a variety of topics, and ensure you are educating in the process.

If you want to entertain or inspire your fans, consider:

- Sharing quotes by great people
- Visualizing data and statistics your company has published in a longer-form post or white paper
- Turning recent customer FAQs into content
- Launching a "Did you know?" series
- Offering tips and lessons
- Featuring industry trends
- Publishing point-of-view posts
- Doing interviews

This is especially critical for B2B companies. The best thing a B2B company can do is focus on helping and adding value to both its customers and its customers' customers through content that helps them be better at their jobs, solve problems, and drive efficiencies.

There's a funny thing that happens when you prioritize helping over selling—you actually sell more! Here's why. By educating and inspiring, you become a trusted company that people follow and subscribe to for content, the company that gets invited to speak at events or conduct workshops. The more you build credibility through helping and adding value, the easier it is to build a tribe that further amplifies your message, creating a powerful halo effect for both your brand and the products or services you offer.

Share Your Creative Journey

As you are developing an idea, a product, or a service, share your creative journey with your communities. It is highly valuable to others to get a glimpse of the process they can learn from.

If You Are a B2B Company, Look at What Your Customers' Customers Care About

In the B2B space, knowing just your customers isn't enough; you need to consider the challenges of their own customers and the possible solutions that might help them address their problems.

The B2B space is tough, especially if you produce unsexy products that make sexy products work. How do you market yourself if you are, well, invisible? General Electric (GE) had a problem making its products and services, such as jet engines and big data sensors, relatable to consumers. The company has expertise in so many fields (aviation, digital, power, global research, healthcare, lighting, transportation, etc.), it was tough to communicate what exactly it does. So GE shifted its marketing strategy toward championing innovation and science in general. It wanted to be seen as a leader in advanced technology rather than just a producer of appliances.

From "Badass Machines" and "DIY Science" boards on Pinterest to celebrating the world's first 3D printing day, GE's campaigns significantly improved awareness and the company's relevance. And who could ignore GE's six-second science experiments on Vine? They were truly works of art!

Then there is emojiscience.com. If you haven't seen it yet, head over there right now and check it out. Another one of my personal favorites is ge-girls.com, "a program designed to encourage girls to explore the world of science, technology, engineering, and math (STEM), and STEM-based careers."

We can keep going with amazing GE examples, but the number of programs and amazing social communities GE maintains quite skillfully doesn't matter. What matters is that by educating, entertaining, and adding value to communities at large, GE truly positioned itself as one of the innovation leaders in the market and earned itself a special place in our hearts.

THE STORYTELLER LAW

Sometimes instead of asking, "Where do we find the stories?" we should be asking "Where do we find the storytellers?" Consider putting the "teller" back into storytelling.

GE's former CMO Beth Comstock talks a lot about the importance of culturally embracing storytelling. A piece of advice she gives brands is to hire people who are "story culture" fits. She says: "All storytellers are not created equal and the thing that separates them is passion. A great storyteller for GE must also love science and have curiosity. Without that combination of passion and curiosity, the beauty of the stories that GE might authentically tell could be lost. Great and visual storytelling isn't about hiring the hottest agency to reshape an image and to make a brand cool. Instead, it's about embracing the inner geek and being true to yourself."

Beth Comstock also suggests developing "story archaeologists." She states: "The brilliant thing about archaeologists is that they don't create history, they only discover it and help us find the meaning behind it. Similarly, there are so many stories that brands have already behind the way they make the things they make. If you can simply get better at finding them more consistently, you can often unlock a hidden treasure of stories that are waiting to be shared."[12]

Another great brand storyteller is a personal friend of ours, Tim Washer. For years he infused his fun-loving personality and humor into Cisco's marketing in his former role as creative director for the Service Provider Group. He now helps other companies do the same as chief creative officer at Ridiculous Media.

Tim is the creator of Cisco's utterly hilarious "A Special Valentine's Day Gift . . . from Cisco!" video to promote its $80,000 ASR 9000 router (you can watch the video here: https://www.youtube.com/watch?v=Z8MWl9UGwQo). A carrier class router is definitely not the traditional Valentine's Day gift for that special person in your life, which is why the humorous video made it to the *New York Times* blog and was widely discussed and shared by marketers and press alike. It is still being talked about now, years later, as an example of how to use humor in great marketing.

Tim Washer is no stranger to comedy. Being a stand-up comedian, Webby-nominated video producer, and corporate humorist, he brings this light touch to all of his work with brands.

I asked him about the thinking behind the video. "We wanted to find a fun way to get some attention with our key influencers, analysts, bloggers, and press," says Washer. "So we thought: wouldn't it be absurd to position our product as the perfect Valentine's Day gift for your lover? And that's what we did."

Tim knew from the outset that the video was unlikely to lead directly to increased router sales: sometimes the selling cycle is 18 to 24 months for a product like this. Someone's not going to stumble across a funny 60-second video and say, "You know what, let's get a couple of these." Instead, he believes in incorporating humor into a wider corporate strategy: "I am a big believer in having a solid global strategy where there's room for white papers, product information, and demos. But at the same time, if you take a very small part of your budget and say, 'Let's just entertain people and give our community the gift of laughter without necessarily a call to action,' others will share your story for you."

Tim's philosophy is that humor elevates a solid marketing message, helping it gain greater exposure. However, a humorous marketing element should still be consistent with the spirit of your brand and the wider themes of your campaigns. "But an occasional humorous video, for example, will help a message stand out among the 100 hours of video content that is uploaded every 60 seconds. A good laugh is a nice gift to give your customers."

Following the success of the Valentine's Day router video, Washer has gone on to use his winning formula in a variety of other notable campaigns. One of his latest gems was the CIO series he produced called "Fast IT and the Slow Waiter" (watch the mock movie trailer here: https://vimeo.com/146670790). In a skit, CIOs from major brands discuss how they are using technology to transform their business. But instead of a typical "talking head" interview, it has an improv approach. Tim plays a dimwitted waiter you might see in an SNL sketch. "The premise was that this waiter was uncomfortably talkative, and that gave us a funny way to bring in the teller and their story," says Washer. "I was totally blown away by how each one was so game to play along with us, and how fun they were." The CIO series won the "Killer Content" award and earned coverage from *CIO* magazine, *The Drum*, and others.

For Tim Washer, making someone laugh is the most intimate connection we can create in a business environment, one that he thinks reflects well on any company. "When a brand shows that it doesn't always take itself too seriously, it's a powerful way to demonstrate authenticity and confidence, as well as connect with your community."

If you want your company to have an authentic and human voice, you need to look within your own storytellers, those who have passion not only for your brand, but for what they do. Develop story archaeologists and cultural storytellers and you won't have to worry about your storytelling well drying up any time soon.

THE LAW OF OPPORTUNITY

Let's talk about the opportunities to infuse your stories with relevant customer interactions.

There are two types of storytelling opportunities:

1. Those that already exist and need to be unearthed
2. Those that pop up unexpectedly and need to be addressed in real time

Let's start with number one. We've already established that a brand is a product of the multiple small gestures it makes every day, during every customer interaction. Look at the customer journey and all of the consumer touchpoints and you'll be able to unearth a ton of marketing ideas that could all make up a consistent and timely brand story.

Examples include:

- Customer communications:
  - E-mails
  - Discount offers
  - Mobile app messages
- Sidewalk and in-store signs
- Event presence
- Website experience
- Blog content (tips, case studies, how-to guides, etc.)
- Customer service interactions
- Partner co-marketing opportunities
- Daily social media communications
- Press releases and company announcements
- Ratings and reviews
- Influencer mentions

- Consumer advocates' blog posts
- Trending industry themes and beyond

The problem is that we often miss the smallest things that could make a big difference. For example, have you thought about spicing up your 404 error web pages? No? Trust us, it's a huge missed opportunity to make your customers smile instead of being irritated with you.

We love Emirates airlines's 404 page, which works beautifully with the rest of the site and fully aligns with the company's brand voice. The message says, "Sorry. We've traveled the globe, but we can't seem to find this page. Continue your journey below." It then offers useful links and a search bar to make it easier for the customer to find similar relevant content. Shutterstock's 404 page features an animation of a child searching under the bed for the page that doesn't exist. And Lego's page showcases different appalled-looking Lego figurines, with one of them unplugging the cord from the outlet.

If you were Dunkin' Donuts or Krispy Kreme, you could have turned the zero in 404 into a colorful donut. Or, include your mascot in the picture. Consider using animation or a video to make it more interactive and fun.

What about the Thank You pages that pop up after your customers subscribe to your communication, download a piece of content, or buy your product? These customers have already bought into your vision. This is an amazing opportunity to capitalize on their attention to offer something else of value, ask for feedback, and more. If someone already went through the effort of subscribing, why not turn it into a memorable experience?

Figure 3.6 is an example of a Thank You page from Scott Monty's personal blog, which appears after you subscribe to his newsletter, "The Full Monty." A former global digital manager for Ford Motor Company and currently CEO and co-managing partner at Brain+Trust Partners, Scott is not only an influential voice in the digital marketing space, but an amazing human being with an authentic voice. It really comes through in the image he uses for his page, as well as the simple and thoughtful copy. It starts with "Seriously – thank you" and ends with the invitation to connect with Scott and share his site with friends. The one thing missing in this otherwise brilliant picture is the signature bow tie Scott is well known for. After all, friends don't let friends miss an opportunity to rock fabulous bow ties.

Even annual reports and shareholder letters present a unique opportunity to do something unconventional.

Calgary Zoo generated national headlines and interest in its annual report by swapping a traditional PDF for Instagram. Proclaiming its 2012 Annual Report "The Year of the Penguins," 55 photos and captions served as the report pages and content, telling the story of what the zoo accomplished over the course of the year in a unique, highly visual way.

Warren Buffett is known for his straightforward and authentic shareholder letters. His annual letters are a brand- and relationship-building tool, a way to humanize his company, Berkshire Hathaway, and show his stakeholders that he is just "one of them" (even though he is one of the wealthiest men on the planet).

How does he turn arguably the driest form of business communication into a pleasant (and at times entertaining) reading experience?

Thank You

Seriously — thank you.

You've taken an additional step that you didn't have to take. You've invited me into your inbox on at least a weekly basis.

The hyper-competitive and constantly interruptive marketplace in which we work makes it difficult for content to rise to the surface these days. But the more intimate setting of email means that you and I will be able to develop a relationship in a less cluttered way.

I'm always open to hearing back from you. If there's something you think I was wrong about, or a piece of content or marketing slip-up that you think needs notice — whatever it is — let me know.

Meanwhile, I'm glad you're here. Feel free to look around. And if you're so inclined, share this site with colleagues and friends. I don't know if they'll be glad that you did, but I sure will be.

Scott

FIGURE 3.6   Scott Monty's Thank You page

First of all, Buffett is honest about the company's successes and failures. When he talks about the successes, it is always in a humble manner. When he talks about his personal oversights, he is not above self-deprecation. In one of his letters, for example, he says:

> Fortunately, my blunders usually involved relatively small acquisitions. Our large buys have generally worked out well and, in a few cases, more than well. I have not, however, made my last mistake in purchasing either businesses or stocks. Not everything works out as planned.

And he gives credit where credit is due:

> In a year in which most equity managers found it impossible to outperform the S&P 500, both Todd Combs and Ted Weschler [handily] did so. Each now runs a portfolio exceeding $7 billion. They've earned it.

> I must confess that their investments outperformed mine. (Charlie says I should add "by a lot.") If such humiliating comparisons continue, I'll have no choice but to cease talking about them.[13]

Buffett's communication style is conversational and no-nonsense; there is no double-talk. And you can always count on humorous one-liners such as this one:

> Charlie and I enjoy issuing Berkshire stock about as much as we relish prepping for a colonoscopy.[14]

Buffett excels at bringing a storytelling approach to business communications. We only wish more shareholder letters were this real and this fun.

These are just some of the examples of existing storytelling opportunities.

Now let's talk a bit about the opportunities that come up in real time. Sometimes you are gifted with golden opportunities not of your own making. You have to take advantage of those, as they don't come along often.

Like when Arby's, a restaurant chain, stole the spotlight during the 2014 Grammys with its hilarious tweet. When singer Pharrell Williams sported a hat that had a great resemblance to Arby's logo, the company had no qualms about seizing the day and tweeted this little gem at him: "Hey @Pharrell, can we have our hat back? #GRAMMYs."[15] To which Pharrell replied: "Y'all tryna start a roast beef?"[16] followed by a smiley face and a kissing emoji. Arby's clever original tweet was an instant hit and was retweeted over 70,000 times, as well as receiving a ton of free press.

Brilliant opportunity, wasn't it? We are glad Arby's didn't miss it so that we could be entertained in the process. However, believe it or not, 95 percent of the time, brands leave those opportunities on the table and don't do anything with them. Such a shame!

Why does that happen? Three main reasons: companies don't listen; they don't care; they are just plain afraid. Listening requires the right infrastructure in place to spot opportunities in real time. Caring takes too much effort: you have to have the right people, process, and playbooks in place to ensure you not only spot the opportunity but respond to it fast in a creative way, and secure all the right approvals internally. You have to be willing to take risks and try new things. All of it requires preparation, planning, and practice. Wow! That's a lot of Ps! Which we'll be happy to explore further in the next chapter.

Chapter 4

THE STORY-MAKING LAWS

CRAFT YOUR STORY

With endless opportunities to uncover compelling stories, how do you craft them for maximum impact?

The previous three chapters all help you to establish the baseline for your brand storytelling strategy. In Chapter 1, you went on a journey of self-reflection by identifying your macro story that defines who you are and what differentiates you. In Chapter 2, you stepped outside of your box to understand how customer, brand, industry, and cultural insights shape your brand storytelling goals and overall strategy. Then in Chapter 3, you went on a creative adventure down the storytelling rabbit hole to brainstorm and map out the types of stories your company could be telling.

You will notice that this chapter has the most laws—12 total—and for good reason! There are a lot of important elements to consider when creating your story. Before you dive in, here is a bit of context so you can make the most of this chapter. The first three laws—the Consistency Law, the Simplicity Law, and the Language Law—all lay the foundation with ground rules to remember. The next six, which run from the Visual Storytelling Law through to the Utility Law, delve into the story-making process and key elements you need to consider as you're creating your macro and micro stories. These are followed by the Ownership Law and the Brand Protection Law to ensure that you understand legal requirements companies need to be aware of. Last, but certainly not least, the Optimization Law rounds out the chapter by showing you how to maximize the success and relatability of your stories.

Are you ready to start crafting your stories?

Let's do this!

THE CONSISTENCY LAW

Consistency is so critical we could probably write a whole other book on the topic.

Consistency is what makes your message clear. Consistency is what helps you build your communities. Consistency is what shapes your reputation. At times, consistency *is* the strategy.

There are different dimensions to consistency:

1. Consistency of behavior
2. Consistency of message

3. Consistency of promise
4. Consistency of engagement
5. Consistency of publishing
6. Consistency of customer care experience

Let's look at each one.

Consistency of behavior is walking the talk, practicing what you preach. Consumers, millennials especially, have a sensitive BS radar. They can spot insincerity or inconsistency between what you say and what you do instantly—and they will call you out on it. There is nowhere to hide. With millions of blogs and billions of social conversations, consumers have no qualms about putting you on the spot and holding you accountable. Consistency of behavior leads to consistency of reputation. Brands need to work hard to earn a great reputation and customers' trust, but it might take only one wrong move to totally destroy it.

Case in point: United Airlines. On its website it has "Our United Customer Commitment" pledge, which states: "We are committed to providing a level of service to our customers that makes us a leader in the airline industry. We understand that to do this we need to have a product we are proud of and employees who like coming to work every day. Our goal is to make every flight a positive experience for our customers."[1]

However, its behavior says otherwise. One of the biggest PR crises of 2017 happened after a passenger was violently dragged off an overbooked United Airlines flight. The video of the incident went viral, and United Airlines's stock plummeted. The company didn't handle the incident well from the start, and this wasn't the only unfortunate episode it was involved in that year. United's consumer perception dropped to a 10-year low.[2]

You can create the sexiest mission statement in the world, but if your behavior doesn't match your message, no amount of aggressive marketing will help you recover your reputation.

Consistency of message ensures that your company is represented as "one brand" across locations, geographies, and product lines. We've talked about the importance of clarity. Even though it isn't the same as lack of confusion, the lack of message consistency can significantly impact customers' perception and understanding of your brand.

Consistency of promise is consistency of execution across locations, channels, and offers. Have you ever walked into a Starbucks trying to redeem an offer only to find out that the staff wasn't even aware of it? You have to ensure not only the consistency of your marketing message, but also the smooth execution of the promises you have made to your customers. Be very clear if certain offers are local or whether or not specific programs apply to a certain subset of your customers.

Consistency of engagement refers to being present and easily accessible to your customers at all times on all channels. Please don't start a community if you are not serious about being a conscious and engaged leader of the community. Don't open a Twitter account if you are only planning on it being a one-way channel for pushing your products. When you give your customers platforms to connect with you, be there! Make it easy for people to reach out and have a conversation with you. And *always* respond. We are not saying you have to be present 24/7. If you are a small business, odds are you won't be checking your messages or social channels every five minutes. In that case, be transparent and share the expected response time. People will appreciate that way more than your silence or a self-serving Facebook page or Twitter account.

Consistency of publishing. To truly build a tribe, you have to consistently create useful and relevant content that engages your communities and keeps you top of mind.

If you ask known bloggers and influencers what is one of the key things that contributes to their success, they will tell you that it's consistency of publishing quality content. If you start a weekly podcast, stick to your schedule and deliver what the audience expects, consistent weekly programming. If you start a blog and you want your community to read it, come back, and engage with you, then make sure you are continuously producing blog posts that spark conversations.

One of the best examples is Seth Godin. Rain or shine, for years now, Seth shares his thoughts with his audience on a daily basis. And he never wavers. He has built a large following not just because of his leadership thinking and thought-provoking content, but because he consistently delivers.

Consistency of customer care experience is making sure that consumers' experience with your brand is the same across all channels (phone, chat, web, social media, in-store, etc.). Not only that, it needs to live up to their expectations based on your marketing messages and company promise.

In recent years customer experience has emerged as the most important priority—and differentiator—for companies large and small. Why? According to Gartner, 89 percent of companies now compete primarily on customer experience.[3] Oftentimes, your product doesn't matter anymore. Nothing is unique; everything can be copied. Great service, however, is a rare thing. Consumers expect companies to know them and serve them when they want, how they want, and on their terms. To compete in this new landscape, companies must shift their focus to making—and keeping—their customers happy. By doing so, brands will benefit more than they ever would from even the most successful marketing campaign.

The stop-and-start mentality is like a disease with brands. Some brands create a great program only to shut it down three months later. They put all of their money into an expensive commercial spot that is totally disconnected from the actual customer experience. They build social communities only to neglect them later.

Consistency leads to clarity, positive sentiment, and good experience. Which, in turn, lead to a great brand reputation, trust, and loyalty. And isn't that what we are all after?

THE SIMPLICITY LAW

Life is short. Attention is a commodity. So: "keep it simple, stupid" (the KISS principle).

It would probably be super cool to just leave it at that and move on to the next section. While the writers in us want to stop, the marketers in us are itching to explore further. Guess who won?

$86 Billion

That is the amount of money brands are leaving on the table when they don't simplify.

No, we didn't make the number up. The data comes from Siegel+Gale's annual Global Brand Simplicity Index that examines the global state of simplicity for the world's leading brands (http://simplicityindex.com). Siegel+Gale looked at a variety of factors from brands' communications to customer interactions. Since 2009, a stock portfolio composed of the simplest publicly traded brands in the global Top 10 has outperformed the major indexes by at least three times.

Here's some additional data from its 2017 report:

- 64 percent of consumers are willing to pay more for simpler experiences
- 61 percent of people are more likely to recommend a brand because it provides simpler experiences and communications
- 62 percent of employees are considered brand champions in companies perceived to be simple versus 20 percent in the companies that are perceived to be complex

Obviously, simplicity pays. And no wonder. We live in an era of limitless choices and information overload. We rebel against technology that's too complicated and menus that are too long. We can catch a quick ride on Uber or Lyft without much hassle. We can transfer money from person to person in seconds via Venmo. We can easily and quickly find an affordable place to stay on Airbnb. These disruptive companies with clear business models and exceptional customer experience are reducing complexity, saving us time, and thus elevating consumer expectations. But most important, these companies are doing it consistently through every single customer touchpoint.

When crafting your story, resist the temptation to overcomplicate. Keep your customer communications and storylines simple, regardless of the channel. Design key messages, quotes, or statements within your story to stand out and be shareable. With this approach, not only will your stories be easier to understand, they will be more memorable.

THE LANGUAGE LAW

It is super easy to default to a stuffy corporate tone in your marketing.

Don't do it.

Look for ways to humanize your brand in everything you do. That starts with the tone of your message.

Remember Warren Buffett's annual shareholder letters earlier in the chapter? They are pretty great, aren't they? Very down to earth, easy to read, and absolutely delightful.

Storyteller brands don't sound like corporate collateral. They speak in a human language.

With tone of voice, it's less about what you say, and more about the way you say it. Your tone of voice brings the character, values, and personality of your business to life and creates an impression on everyone who reads or hears your message. It can become a powerful secret sauce, differentiating your brand from others.

The brands with the best and most authentic tone of voice are the ones that really know who they are and what makes them special. These brands also deeply understand how their customers perceive them, plus customers' needs, wants, and wishes. The secret sauce comes from translating these insights, values, and key differentiators into a communication style that banishes boring in favor of personality.

We're not saying that every brand has to be quirky or display a level of humor rivaling that of a stand-up comedian. That's not realistic. The devil is in the details here. GE proudly takes a stand on issues it believes in, like getting more women into STEM (science, technology, engineering, and mathematics) careers. However, it also uses its Pinterest board to express its passion for "Badass Machines" and share Thomas Edison Valentine's Day memes, personifying a coolness factor rarely found in companies in its industry.

And remember how Dunkin' Donuts incorporated its famous DDs into worDDs strategically (see what we did there)? By playfully celebrating its customers' love for coffee, donuts, and breakfast foods in a human yet upbeat tone of voice, Dunkin's willingness to go the extra mile makes a big difference in how its customers perceive the company.

Let's dig deeper into a few clever ways companies can ditch the corporate speak in favor of a tone of voice that is all their own.

Be the Voice Customers Want to Hear— Even When They Cannot Sleep

Casper, a mattress company on a quest to engineer better sleep, is a prime example of a brand that has nailed its tone of voice. Casper entered the market as a disruptor. Simplicity rules: the company launched with only one mattress option (it now has three varieties, plus supplemental product such as pillows, sheets, etc.).

What truly differentiates Casper is its friendly, conversational, and sometimes tongue-in-cheek take on the topic of sleep. From the first bit of copy on the company's website, "Better sleep, better everything," to its news announcements, "Breaking Snooze," Casper consistently celebrates all things sleep in a personable way.

This strategy extends across all of the brand's online and offline touchpoints. Casper's blog (http://blog .casper.com/), which used to be lovingly called Pillow Talk and is now renamed Casper the Blog, offers solutions like "Can't Sleep? Try These 12 Things to Bore You to Bed," and information you didn't realize you wanted such as, "How Foam Mattresses Work, According to a Chemical Engineer."

In addition to its blog, Casper runs a lifestyle magazine called *Woolly Magazine* (https://woollymag.com/), covering wellness topics its community cares about like, "Why You Should Spend Valentine's Day Alone" and "Is the Man Flu Really a Thing?"

Casper has also won the hearts of its sleep-loving community on social media. The company's tweets are conversational yet irreverent, with lines like, "We're all just pillowcases looking for our pillows,"[4] or "Today is gonna be a no for us."[5] Simple yet highly relatable, the company's tone of voice is reflective of the conversations you might have with friends. This even extends to customer service tweets, where the company responded with a meme of a man saying, "Noooooooooo" to a customer who had not received a mattress that was shown to have been delivered. The response continues, "Send us a DM with your order # so we can look into this for you."[6]

Casper also uses social media to cater to its customers' needs—just not quite in the way you would expect. For customers who want to stay cozy at home, while still maintaining the all-important image that their social life is "lit," Casper's Late Night Snap Hacks have them covered. Hosted on a dedicated microsite (http://latenightsnaphacks.com/), scenes include everything from a disco ball to people dancing at a club or driving through the streets of New York City. Customers can put their phone up to the screen and record it for Snapchat to create the illusion of a rockin' night out. And, before you judge, you know we have all been there at one point in our lives!

For its insomniac customers, Casper launched the Insomnobot-3000 (http://insomnobot3000.com/), a chatbot that is described as "A friendly, easily distracted bot designed to keep you company when you just can't fall asleep. Extra chatty between 11pm and 5am. U up? then text 844-823-5621."[7]

According to Lindsay Kaplan, Casper's VP of communications and brand engagement, "We knew when we started that we were up against a big oligarchy, with all the massive corporations—pardon the pun—in bed together. Our strategy from the start has been on changing perceptions about mattress shopping and creating a community around sleep in a playful and creative way, with a genuine voice."[8]

This extends offline. The company has opened stores across the United States where you can book a "nap appointment" and test out its mattress. In 2016, the company hosted its first-ever Sleep Symposium, an eye-opening day of conversations and experiences exploring the culture of sleep, featuring noteworthy speakers including Arianna Huffington, plus experiences such as a guided meditation, a virtual reality spa, and even an illustrator drawing dreams.[9]

Casper's box and packaging were also designed to differentiate the brand. The mattress comes in a box the size of a mini fridge. Because the experience of unboxing a Casper mattress is so different, it has spawned a series of customer videos on YouTube. After removing all of the packaging and plastic, the company encourages customers to listen to the mattress "sigh with relief" as it unrolls and expands to its full size.

Casper's goal is to be the "first end-to-end brand around all things sleep," and while its products deliver according to its mission, it's the company's quirky personality, tone of voice, and consistent customer experience that have brought it into so many customers' minds—and bedrooms.

Tap Employee Advocates to Tell Your Story—in Their Words

Leveraging employee advocates offers another way to humanize your company's tone of voice and message. Inspired to showcase the authentic culture at Cisco around the globe and attract new talent, the company launched the #WeAreCisco initiative.

Through social listening and sourcing stories for the company's Life at Cisco blog, the company identified a core team of employee brand evangelists to launch dedicated @WeAreCisco Facebook, Twitter, Instagram, and Snapchat channels for the brand. While the accounts are run by the company's Talent Brand Social Team, employees volunteer to manage specific channels like Snapchat or Instagram stories on specific days, sharing unique stories and content from their perspective.

Since their launch, the @WeAreCisco channels have featured almost entirely employee-generated content. The company actively monitors the #WeAreCisco hashtag for employee posts and reaches out directly to ask for permission to use these, plus the original photo or video on social media, crediting employees if they are OK with being tagged.[10]

@WeAreCisco has had millions of minutes of Snapchat stories viewed, with an average Snapchat story completion rate of between 60 and 70 percent. The company's efforts have also inspired collaborations with NASDAQ and the Grace Hopper Celebration of Women Conference.[11]

What's brilliant about #WeAreCisco is how the company creates a culture that rewards employee advocacy. Too often, companies are scared for employees to share their stories and feedback in a very public form. Not Cisco. Cisco knows that it has a good culture, and its advocacy initiative encourages employees to "be you, with us."[12]

In addition to its social media efforts, the company's Life at Cisco blog is composed of posts bylined by employees. The team behind it credits social media as the top way to uncover these stories. The Life at Cisco blog is the second most popular blog at Cisco, behind its Network news site.

Look closely at the Life at Cisco blog (https://blogs .cisco.com/lifeatcisco), and you will see a theme. From career-focused content, with employees reflecting on their professional journeys, to quirkier fare, such as how the company celebrated May the 4th, which is known to fans as Star Wars Day, the stories showcase the many unique people, interests, and talents behind the mega brand.

At an internal, all-employee meeting (the Cisco Beat), during the "Ask the Execs Anything" session, one Star Wars-obsessed employee asked if Cisco would consider a companywide #Maythe4th celebration. Not only did the company's CEO Chuck Robbins respond with "absolutely," he nominated a fellow Star Wars fan on the company's executive leadership team as the perfect "rebel" to lead the "alliance." Inspired by this and other employees' love for #Maythe4th, the company ran an Instagram contest asking employees to showcase how they were leveraging the Cisco Force, to celebrate innovation and technology.[13] From donning Star Wars costumes, to posing with life-sized cardboard cutouts of the franchise's characters or imagining what would happen if the Empire had a Cisco Spark Board, creative geekery was literally a force to be reckoned with![14]

Examples like this, plus the personal stories from Cisco employees, humanize the brand and influence public perception. When employees volunteer to take over a Cisco-branded social media channel, they are not provided a script. They must sign off on the social media policy, but that's it. They are encouraged to use their own voices, versus trying to mimic Cisco's brand voice. By doing this at scale, the different employee voices are actually shaping Cisco's tone of voice and stories. Which, for a brand that is largely perceived as more corporate, has become an incredibly effective way to shatter that perception.

Furthermore, the halo effect from its employee advocacy efforts goes far beyond hiring. Research from LinkedIn shows that content shared by employees has two times higher engagement versus content shared by a company.[15] By building and cultivating a culture of sharing stories about what it is like to work at Cisco, the company also improves its image among clients, prospects, and other influencers in its industry. People want to do business with individuals and companies that they like and trust.

Partner with Innovators to Infuse Personality into Brand Storytelling

If we had a dollar for every slick automotive video, website, and social media campaign, well, we would be very wealthy women. Yet, in a sea of engine revs, impossibly shiny paint jobs, and hairpin roads to traverse, one automotive ad stands out. And no, it's not for the latest Ferrari. It's for David Johns's 1999 Holden Barina. For those wondering what a Holden Barina is, it's a compact automobile sold by an Australian car manufacturer called Holden, which became part of General Motors in 2005.

When David decided it was time to sell his beloved Barina, he knew that it wasn't going to be easy. The car had 188,000+ kilometers on the odometer, only three hubcaps, and its share of dents and scratches. David had an aha moment. Despite its drawbacks, the car also came with quite a few positives. For example, it will move you—literally. Plus, it had ample storage, so ample that it could easily fit the vehicle's exhaust—you know, should the need arise. Also, it came from a lovely, always garaged home with owners who wanted to see it go to someone who would cherish it like they had.

David, who happened to work for a video production company, pitched a wacky idea to his colleagues: let's bring the Barina to life in the most epic used car sales video ever. They came up with the clever tagline, "Don't just make history—drive it."[16]

You should definitely watch it before you read on: https://youtu.be/BJj7Km7Raks.

The video opens with David behind the wheel, turning on the Barina while the copy, "One careful owner," flashes across the screen. Images of the car's less-than-sleek exterior follow with text that calls out, "10 months rego (a vehicle tax in Australia)," "Always garaged," and "Matching seats."

The car's lights dramatically turn on while David, looking rather James Bond-esque in a suit and sunglasses, revs the engine and takes the Barina for a spin. The words "Performance redefined," "Style," and "Luxury" appear on the screen before it cuts to David holding the keys, with the line, "It could be yours." A call-to-action then flashes on the screen to tweet David an offer with the hashtag #BuyMyBarina.

In under five days, David's mission to sell his 1999 Barina had reached a global audience. He received valid offers of $1,000 and $2,000 (double the asking price), and a few wackier ones.

> @ThenamesT tweeted, "I will offer you a box of crackerjacks and a gently used loofa #buymybarina."
>
> @Gnutian offered, "Hi, I will offer you a handful of orange LEGO, 3 blue pastel post-its and a fish for your awesome Barina #BuyMyBarina."
>
> @iamhaska kept it real, saying, "I have no use for a car, but I MUST HAVE this one #BuyMyBarina. And the sexy Aussie that comes with it! <3"

We like your style, @iamhaska!

Then the unexpected happened. Australia's NRMA Insurance made David an offer he could not refuse. NRMA Insurance, a company that offers a range of automotive and home insurance solutions, wanted to buy the car. David accepted and donated the money to Cancer Council Australia.

Robert McDonald, head of research at NRMA Insurance, said, "We are very excited to have purchased the car for such a great cause. As part of our road safety research program, we regularly test new and older vehicles and we have some special plans for this little car."[17]

Robert was not kidding. The company wanted to parlay the Barina's fame into telling a story about the work the NRMA Insurance Research Centre carries out with physical testing, data analysis, consumer advisory on car safety, and comprehensive car insurance reduction.

That sounds so corporate, right? And the messaging was—until the Barina and NRMA Insurance came together. David and his team partnered with NRMA Insurance to craft a story of epic proportions in a follow-up video.

The NRMA Insurance video starts with David, still dressed in the same suit, handing the keys over to the company's secret testing and research lab. David casts a worried look at the lab team. They assure him that they're only going to "run a few tests," and ask, "What could possibly go wrong?"

As the R&D team gets to work, the little Barina's results are off the charts. Everyone is confused. Something is not right. As the team reruns the tests, a freak accident turns the beloved Barina into

"BARINAGEDDON." With a mutant car now on the loose, the Barina is out to show the world what it is capable of.

Sound fantastic, if not a bit out there? Watch the full video and judge for yourself: https://youtu.be/kStwTFMTfYs.

There are a few great takeaways from #BuyMyBarina. First and foremost, it resonated because it dared to be different. How many bland or eerily similar automotive ads have you seen? They all blur together. The boldness and humor caught people's attention. The notion of loving an old car despite its faults is highly relatable. It also created an experience for people around the world who read and submitted "offers" for the vehicle.

Second, kudos to NRMA Insurance for jumping on board. We love how NRMA Insurance took the Barina's success story and leveraged it to showcase the work it does in its R&D lab. Sure, the example is sensational and akin to a superhero movie, but that's part of the brilliance! Especially when you're in an industry that's more formal, telling your story in a fun, creative way differentiates you from your competitors. Plus, partnerships offer a great opportunity to amplify your brand voice and test innovative ways to tell exciting stories that resonate with your customers.

THE VISUAL STORYTELLING LAW

Imagine this: you're waiting for your subway train. Just as it arrives, a seemingly static billboard of a young woman with long hair comes to life, and her hair starts to blow around. It's as if the wind generated by the train's arrival is propelling the movement of her hair in real time.

However, as the train starts to slow down, the wind blowing the woman's hair only becomes stronger. And then the unexpected happens—her hair (which was actually a wig) blows off and exposes her bald head. We can only guess what happens next: your surprise and smile are likely replaced by a shocked expression. You are stunned, trying to figure out what just happened.

As you have probably guessed, this is no ordinary billboard. It was created by the Swedish Childhood Cancer Foundation to showcase the everyday reality children with cancer face.

The billboard's animation ends with the message "Every day a child is diagnosed with cancer," and invites you to text a specific number to donate to the foundation.

A video released by the nonprofit captured the powerful reactions to the billboard from people on the train platform, expressing their shock and sadness: https://youtu.be/064ipuBiWDg.

As the video was shared across social networks and news media, it sparked a strong response, not just in Sweden, but around the world. The foundation's innovative use of cutting-edge technology in its visual storytelling successfully raised awareness and funds for childhood cancer.

While there are many ways to craft the story's narrative, the visuals were what brought the story to life in a powerful way. The right visuals appeal to human emotions and make a story memorable.

Visual storytelling is defined as the use of images, videos, infographics, presentations, and other visual elements to craft a story around key brand values and offerings.

We are now marketing in an era of "infobesity," where consumers are faced with more messages across more channels than ever before. Visual storytelling, when done correctly, is a powerful strategy for standing out.

The reason is simple. As humans, we are wired to process visual information more efficiently:

- Visuals are processed 60,000 times faster than text by the human brain[18]
- 90 percent of information transmitted to the brain is visual[19]
- People can recall 65 percent of the visual content that they see almost three days later, compared to 10 percent of written content[20]

Given this information, it's easy to see how all elements across the digital and social media spectrum, from websites to e-mail to status updates, have become increasingly visual. Even the social networks think visual and mobile first, all completing redesigns to prioritize images, videos, GIFs, and more. Why? It's what people want. On Snapchat alone, users send 3 billion snaps every day, while Facebook users watch over 100 million hours of video on the platform daily.[21]

Combine people's passion for visuals with a love for stories and it's akin to mesmerizing fireworks exploding in the sky. People love stories because they're inherently more personal. Whether we are revealing something about ourselves or sharing humorous memories or heartwarming discoveries, stories spark an emotional response. So much so that research from Stanford University has found that stories are 22 times more memorable than facts alone.[22]

In the age of "infobesity," where consumers are faced with more messages across more channels than ever before, visual storytelling has emerged as a powerful strategy to help marketers stand above the noise and grow a vibrant and engaged community.

For companies to cut through the clutter, they need to focus on creating and curating the best quality content that offers value to their consumers and brings them into the conversation. Leveraging visual storytelling allows businesses not only to get noticed, but to truly connect with their audiences.

However, you should be strategic about your approach.

First, your visuals should reflect your definitive signature. You have obsessed over your logo, your colors, and your design style. A key to standing out in a crowded newsfeed is to ensure that your visuals are also reflective of your visual identity. Look closely at what constitutes your definitive signature, whether it's colors, your logo, or a symbolic image like Baskin-Robbins's pink spoon or McDonald's golden arches, and think about how to use these to work in harmony with the visual stories you want to tell.

For example, when Boston-area company GotVMail wanted to rebrand itself as Grasshopper, the company turned to video. Grasshopper, which promotes itself as the entrepreneur's phone system, created an inspirational video for its YouTube channel called "Entrepreneurs can change the world" (https://www.youtube.com/watch?v=T6MhAwQ64c0).

The video was simple, yet powerful in its design, pairing Grasshopper's signature bright green with a text overlay that reads, "Do you remember when you were a kid and you thought you could do anything?" The video then uses text, visuals and inspiring music to bring its message to life. After watching the video for the first time—we'll admit it—we were a bit emotional because it is an honest yet powerful reminder of why it's so special to be an entrepreneur.

The video was shared online and in a direct mail package that included a press release and edible, chocolate-covered grasshoppers to key influencers and the news. Knowing that entrepreneurs have a high propensity for risk, the recipients were challenged to try the chocolate-covered grasshoppers.

Grasshopper's bold mailing and inspiring video made for an unforgettable duo. With more than 1.1 million views on YouTube, the video became a viral sensation and started a movement.[23] As a result of the initiative, Grasshopper significantly grew the company's social media communities, secured multiple national TV placements, and successfully drove traffic to the company's website.

Grasshopper's rebranding campaign is a fantastic reminder of how powerful visual storytelling can be. By telling the story of its mission—empowering entrepreneurs—in an inspiring way through video, Grasshopper sparked significant awareness with its target audience and differentiated the company in the market. As this was a rebrand, elements such as the use of the new company colors and chocolate-covered grasshoppers crystallized the company's definitive signature.

Following the success of the campaign, the best practice would be to continue to leverage these distinct elements across the design of your visuals, as it would make your brand more eye-catching in a crowded newsfeed. We find it hard to believe that the individuals who were brave enough to eat the chocolate-covered grasshopper will ever forget this campaign, but for others who might have only seen the video, consistently putting your unique stamp on each visual storytelling initiative is key to sustaining momentum after a breakout success.

Second, you have to marry content with context.

We have a strange question for you: how many times does your job require reminding the visitors to your office that toy grenades are not allowed in the workplace?

For most of us, never. But if you are the TSA, this is a daily occurrence.

To educate travelers about what they cannot pack in their hand luggage at the airport, the government agency has taken to Instagram to shine a spotlight on the weird and sometimes scary things people deem OK to pack. While it seems obvious not to pack a bejeweled lipstick taser, ninja throwing stars, or an iPhone case that doubles as a Swiss army knife, the reality, as shown by the TSA on social media, is that travelers actually do—often. On the TSA's Instagram, each image of a confiscated item comes with a story about when and where the item was discovered, plus a reminder why those items are not allowed.

In a recent post showcasing a pink dinosaur grenade toy (that's a thing?!), the TSA wrote, "While one might say that this pink plastic dinosaur-shaped grenade is dino-mite, it's not permitted in carry-on or checked baggage. Yeah, I know . . . It's a pink plastic toy. But as I've explained before, anything that resembles a grenade is not permitted. At all. Jurassic'n for a bag search if you pack one. This one was discovered by a TSA officer (not a paleontologist) in a carry-on bag at Denver (DEN)."[24]

The images are shared as they are confiscated, adding relevance to the stories. It's one thing to be told that you cannot pack toy grenades, quite another to see a visual of one that someone tried to bring on board last week! The mix of unexpected items, plus the light-hearted copy, brings the story to life. It shows the great work done by the TSA, while reinforcing its policies.

The TSA takes its efforts one step further on Twitter with its @AskTSA account. Customers can tweet their questions or images of items to see if they're OK to bring in their checked or carry-on bags. The initiative has increased engagement with travelers and jokesters alike, with one fan of the account tweeting an image of a human-sized inflatable dinosaur, asking, "Can we bring our dinosaur on a plane? He doesn't bite. Much." To which the TSA playfully responded, "Jurassic'n me what? Your dinosaur would have to be placed in the cargo hold because, well, he's a dinosaur . . . But also because he wouldn't be able to raise his arms in the body scanner."[25]

Seriously, what is with dinosaurs and airport security?!

Jokes aside, the TSA's strategy reinforces that visual storytelling is more than just selecting the right images. The context of the platforms on which you share your content is critical. For the TSA, Instagram is a valuable awareness platform. There are tons of "OMG moments" from the super random items confiscated that pique people's curiosity to tune in regularly. Adding the more interactive element on Twitter to ask very specific questions via text or image offers a valuable customer service to those who would otherwise be too shy or don't have time to call the TSA directly.

We are still keeping our fingers crossed for a TSA Tumblr page. Can you imagine what they could do with GIFs? #yesplease.

With the vast majority of channels prioritizing visuals, the best practice is to evaluate the channels your customers love and frequent. Look closely at how they consume, share, and engage by platform. For most companies, customer preferences vary by platform. Each channel has strategic features to maximize visual storytelling opportunities. However, it's worth noting that it's not just about social media. In Chapter 5, we will discuss everything—your packaging, website, mobile apps, voice assistants, and more—that can be leveraged for brand and visual storytelling.

We are so passionate about the topic of visual storytelling, we could literally write a whole separate book about it. Oh wait, we already did! Our previous book, *The Power of Visual Storytelling*, dives deeper into the importance of using videos, images, and other visual formats in your content strategy. We discuss the range of visual mediums that are ripe for storytelling, top channels to maximize, and a step-by-step road map to build a visual storytelling strategy and program for your business.

THE DIVERSIFICATION LAW

When developing your visual storytelling strategy, it's easy to default to images and videos. While those are the "classics," the magic truly is in the visual mix. From infographics to cinemagraphs, presentations, and more, each visual brings something unique to the table, offering companies different ways to bring their stories to life.

With more visual opportunities than ever before at our fingertips, let's dig deeper into how to maximize some of the popular mediums for visual storytelling:

- Cartoons
- Cinemagraphs
- GIFs
- Images
- Infographics
- Memes
- Presentations
- White papers and e-books
- Videos

Cartoons

Raise your hand if you would like to triple the level of engagement with your audience.

Well, that's exactly what you'll get if you use cartoons as a medium.

We have been longtime fans of cartoons as a way to deliver a message in a unique and relevant way. Why? Because it resonates. Because people like to laugh. Because it's authentic. And quite honestly because it's still new and unique; not a lot of brands have been smart enough to tap into this format. Yet. Those that have, however, are seeing great results.

We reached out to one of the most brilliant marketing artists, Tom Fishburne, who is known in the industry as Marketoonist (www.marketoonist.com). "Branded content rarely passes the bedtime story test," Tom told us, "let alone a cluttered Facebook stream, Twitter feed, or Pinterest board. Cartoons do. They are the classical visual storytelling medium. For generations, readers have stuck them to refrigerators and tacked them to office walls."

Tom says most of the brands he works with use cartoons as a top-of-the-funnel awareness-driving tactic. They are looking to reach the audiences that are very hard to break through to and interact with. "To be able to not only engage these audiences, but to triple the engagement compared to using other types of media is very compelling to them," says Tom. "Especially if they want to engage these communities consistently because cartoons are great at capturing that interest."

Cartoons are fantastic at keeping that interest long-term as well. Brands that use cartoons on a regular cadence not only see spikes in the initial engagement, but see sustained interest over time because the audience looks forward to the next installment. It's a self-perpetuating cycle.

One of our favorite Marketoonist campaigns was Tom's partnership with LinkedIn. The company encouraged users to update their LinkedIn profiles through its Banish the Buzzwords campaign. The team did some research and ranked the most commonly used buzzwords on LinkedIn profiles around the world. Then they created a series of cartoons highlighting the inherent humor of those buzzwords: each cartoon visualized situations in which the most common buzzwords were used in real life (Figure 4.1). LinkedIn then aggregated these cartoons in a SlideShare presentation along with tips on updating your profile (https://www.slideshare.net/linkedin/buzzwords-2016).

The series was translated into a dozen languages and syndicated across earned and paid social channels, and more than tripled expected engagement rates.

Many companies are starting to explore engaging their internal employee audiences in unique ways as well. Schneider Electric is one example. With 160,000 employees around the world, the company wanted to spark conversations internally about cultural values. It worked with Tom to create a series of cartoons about issues such as communication, talent management, and inspiring teams. Because the cartoons were particular to its organization, they really struck a chord with employees and ignited conversations worldwide.

Simple. Fun. Brilliant.

Cinemagraphs

Cinemagraphs are exciting to brand storytellers and advertisers alike because of their format: a GIF/video hybrid in which a static image has one video element that plays in a never-ending loop, resulting in constant motion. The unexpected motion is equal parts creative and eye-catching, allowing a brand to shine a spotlight on a key feature or element.

FIGURE 4.1   Select cartoons from
Banish the Buzzwords campaign

For example, when I (Jessica) was working with Magners Cider, my agency team developed a cinemagraph showcasing someone outside on a beautiful day pouring the beverage into a glass filled with ice (the way it should be enjoyed). With the liquid pouring into the glass on a never-ending loop, the cinemagraph was designed to pull the viewer in and spark cravings for that refreshing first sip of Magners Cider.

This type of visual stands out in a cluttered newsfeed. At a time when you have between 2.8 and 8 seconds to capture someone's attention, it's easy to see why more brands are using cinemagraphs in their visual content mix.

The elegance of cinemagraphs has also made them a favorite format among luxury brands such as Chanel, Balenciaga, and Stuart Weitzman that use it to highlight details of clothing, perfume, and shoes respectively. GE has employed cinemagraphs to show machines in motion, while Honda has utilized them to provide a sneak peek of a new automobile.

Cinemagraphs are also alluring for advertisers, as the never-ending loop means they can tap into Instagram's and Facebook's autoplay capabilities. Microsoft tested cinemagraphs in a series of ads promoting its Surface products on Facebook and Twitter. It saw a 110 percent increase in engagement on Twitter, compared to a 1.96 percent increase in engagement from ads using still photos, and an 85 percent increase in engagement rates on Facebook, versus a 0.83 percent increase with the still image ads.[26]

GIFs

Here's a fun fact for your next cocktail party: GIFs have actually been around since 1987. GIF, which stands for graphics interchange format, allow designers to store multiple images or still frames from a video in an image file, bringing the image to life with animation.

Although GIFs seem to be a relatively simple format at first glance, what makes this visual medium special is its ability to tell a bite-sized story in a few seconds. Some of the most famous GIFs to date include President Obama's famous mic drop at his final White House Correspondents' Dinner in 2016 and Peggy Olson's epic hallway walk on Mad Men. Whether it's an action or a funny one-liner, many GIFs reflect iconic or hilarious pop culture moments.

With GIFs now usable across multiple social media and digital channels, consider building a library of situational GIFs related to your company. It could be a funny reaction from your CEO, footage of your products, or scenes of your company mascot. The key is to use the GIF to tell a quick story or convey a relatable emotion or moment.

One creative visual storytelling initiative using GIFs is Lime-A-Rita's "Meet the Ritas" campaign. Starring three sassy brand ambassadors, the Ritas, lounge poolside with Lime-A-Rita's canned margaritas in hand while doling out social media advice and gossip to fans who engage with the brand on Twitter, Instagram, or Facebook using the hashtag #RitaSays. While images, videos, and memes feature prominently on Facebook and Instagram, GIFs are the star of the show on Twitter.

In response to Justin, who tweeted, "@TheRitas are any of you single? asking for a friend . . ." the Ritas cheekily responded, "Sorry. No one cuts in line for the slip n' slide. Not even 'special friends'" #RitaSays.[27] A GIF features the Ritas sassily posing on a Slip 'N Slide.

We could be biased, but quite possibly *the best* response from the Ritas comes from our question to the ladies. After a long (but happy!) day of writing, I (Jessica) playfully took a jab at Ekaterina, asking @TheRitas, "Any advice on the best ratio of work/play? I need to have a conversation with a colleague who is cracking the whip (err . . . @ekaterina) #ritasays."[28]

Not only did the Ritas respond, their response was epic: "Shoot for a 25/75 ratio. Work until you're 25, party until you're 75. And then some. #RitaSays."[29]

Someone please find us the GIF of the President Obama mic drop ASAP!

For those who don't know, the 25/75 ratio referenced is a play on the classic 3:2:1 ratio for making a margarita, which translates to 3 parts tequila, 2 parts Cointreau, and 1 part lime juice. Well played, ladies!

Bringing a sassy social media advice column to life with GIFs is just the slushy top of the frozen margarita. Here are some GIF-worthy ideas to inspire you:

- **Products.** GIFs can help accentuate key features or showcase how a product works in a fun, engaging way.
- **Events.** Highlight a key moment from an event, whether it's a quote, feature, or funny occurrence.
- **Behind the scenes.** Offer fans a window into your office culture. Whether it's a monthly ice cream sundae party or celebrating a big moment, GIFs can make these small but meaningful moments pop.
- **#TBT.** Add animation to your #TBT by bringing historic imagery to life in a GIF.
- **Quotes and statements.** GIFs can imbue quotes and statements with emotion.

Memes

From *Game of Thrones* references to hilarious imaginary conversations between Barack Obama and Joe Biden or the ever-famous Grumpy Cat, memes often go viral and serve as signifiers of the spread of cultural information.

While memes are often inspired by current events, pop culture moments, or jokes, there's no reason why companies cannot also tap into the format's humorous powers to tell their stories.

IKEA Singapore's Shelf Help Guru campaign offers a clever example of how to leverage memes as part of an integrated campaign. The company introduced a quirky yet inspiring character called Fille Güte, a "Shelf Help Guru," to educate consumers on how to have a happy home. Introduced in a humorous YouTube video, Fille advises that, "The key to a happy home is a happy private life," and "When you unlock the doors to your most private areas, happiness can enter" (https://www.youtube.com/watch?v=Tmv8rCd_NiA).

In case you're wondering (because we know you are!), the private areas Fille refers to in the video are actually your bedroom and bathroom. Whether things are getting complicated in the bedroom or painful in the bathroom, Fille takes IKEA customers through a series of relatable, yet cheeky scenarios filled with double entendres.

For example, a scene plays out between a husband and wife, where the wife looks frustratingly at her husband and says, "I just wish you knew what to do with your junk." He stares back at her in horror, and then looks down at the mess on the floor before acknowledging, "I think we need a little space." His wife agrees, and the video then showcases a transformed bedroom and a happy couple with ample amounts of storage space from IKEA.

While the video is clever and full of fabulous furniture-related puns, IKEA Singapore didn't stop there. On its Facebook page it hosted a contest offering fans a chance to win a $50 gift card for submitting a question to the Shelf Help Guru about how to improve their private lives.

Expectedly, it received a slew of wacky questions. The team responded to each one with a funny meme starring the Shelf Help Guru, and including a link to the relevant Ikea product page, such as:

- Fille sitting at the foot of a bed with the caption, "If you can't decide, sleep on it."
- Fille in a bathrobe with the shower curtain and the text, "Always draw the curtain on private matters."
- Fille sitting next to a lamp with the line, "Some things are such a turn-on."

The memes expand in a humorous and memorable way the story of Fille, the Shelf Help Guru, told in the video. A visual response feels more special and is ultimately more shareable, showcasing that next-level content opportunities are not limited to a status update. The campaign also speaks to how companies shouldn't be afraid to get personal with their customers, even if it means poking a little fun at yourself.

Succeeding in today's social media environment calls for creating positive experiences for your customers. Community managers do this each and every day, but this campaign is a good reminder of just how valuable their efforts are—and the details that go into executing them flawlessly.

Infographics

Infographics bring together the best of data and visuals to tell a story. Offering a visual representation of information, infographics help companies emphasize key points while packaging content in a highly shareable way.

From social media sites like Facebook, Twitter, and Pinterest, to e-mail, websites, blogs, and news outlets, one infographic can get a lot of mileage. Additionally, when designed well, infographics can enhance thought leadership, educate a target audience, and optimize search engine rankings.

Infographics play a prominent role in B2B marketing. Jobvite, a recruitment software solution that helps companies source, hire, and onboard top talent, strategically uses infographics to educate, spark conversations, and share best practices on topics that are important to its customer base. In a highly creative infographic called "The Search for the Pink Unicorn," Jobvite describes this mythical creature as an "A-list candidate . . . a rare breed" that "can be tricky to catch." The infographic then goes into "how to entice—*and hang on to*—this sought-after prize."[30] The company has also played off trending topics like the law of attraction, with an infographic on "The Law of Employee Attraction." It also features its own products in infographics, with one on "Continuous Candidate Engagement™—Why You Need CCE."[31]

With infographics, design is the main differentiator. Your brand's definitive signature should be present, from the colors or icons you use to how you phrase any supporting copy. The best infographics have a natural flow and take the viewer along a desired path to the story or key message. Start with a headline that clearly communicates the topic you will be covering. Then identify the problem. What is your infographic helping to address or solve for? Supporting data points should follow in a simple, easy-to-read flow. End with a conclusion that offers a high-level summary and a call to action.

Presentations

Digital and social media have reinvented how we look at presentations. No longer just for conferences, speeches, and business meetings, companies are now curating highly visual presentations to bring stories, ideas, quotes, and tips to life. And with channels like SlideShare, presentations are now embeddable across a range of websites and blogs.

The key to successful visual storytelling through presentations is to consider them opportunities for thought leadership and consumer engagement. Ask yourself, what content or stories can you capture in a highly visual format to inspire, motivate, entertain, or teach? Whether it's frequently asked customer questions, your company's core values or mission, inspiring quotes, or a how-to from an internal expert, there are so many opportunities for leveraging presentations creatively.

One example we love of a company that regularly develops innovative presentations is Experian. Every Wednesday at 3:00 p.m., Experian hosts a #CreditChat focused on money and personal finance issues that matter to its consumers. The chat features a different group of people each time, including a range of financial industry experts, influencers, journalists, and Experian employees. The chat is hosted live across Periscope, YouTube Live, Twitter, and Snapchat. The Experian team also posts presentations from past chats on SlideShare. One #CreditChat presentation, "How to Save on Holiday Travel," was 65 pages long and has been viewed over 78,000 times since it was posted in December 2015.[32] Each slide is clean and easy to read, featuring the answer to a question discussed during the chat. With the ability to clip slides from the #CreditChat, Experian can evaluate which tips and slides are the most popular, inspiring future opportunities to create personalized content around them.

The goal of the weekly #CreditChat is to offer valuable insights and expert tips to help its current and prospective customer base to become more financially capable. Chats take place across a range of channels, allowing the Experian team to connect directly with people on an individual level on the channel each prefers to spend time on. The initiative reaches millions of people weekly while positioning Experian as a trusted advisor on personal finance.

White Papers and E-books

With the goals of thought leadership and lead generation particularly in the B2B space, white papers and e-books have become go-to mediums to feature educational content and interviews with experts on a dedicated topic. The key with both mediums is to bring the white paper or e-book to life with visuals. Not only are visuals attention-grabbing, but when paired strategically with text, they make key points more memorable and content more "sticky," while keeping the reader engaged for longer.

Not to be outdone by their B2B counterparts, several B2C companies have dabbled in the e-book space. KFC debuted its first romance novella, *Tender Wings of Desire*, on Mother's Day. Featuring Harland Sanders as the love interest, the book was made available on Amazon as a free download or free with a $20 "Fill Up" featuring KFC's Extra Crispy Chicken.[33]

If your brand truly aspires to leverage the e-book format for visual storytelling purposes, consider taking a page from Land Rover's playbook. Land Rover partnered with British novelist and screenwriter William Boyd to release *The Vanishing Game*, a 17,000-word novel available on Tumblr and iBooks for free.

It tells the story of a driving adventure from London to the southern tip of Skye in Scotland, and features Land Rover as a supporting character that transports the protagonist, Alec Dunbar, to his final destination. It takes the majority of the first chapter to even mention the vehicle, let alone see a visual of it.

Originally hosted on Tumblr (it's sadly no longer live), the end result was a sensory yet surprising experience that serves as a great reminder for brands to cater to their customers by prioritizing unique content over product placement. Moving graphics and still images brought the novel to life. Music and a voiceover narrative seamlessly synced with the text overlay, adding an experiential layer to the novel that was completely different from that of a traditional e-book.[34]

The Visual Nuances: Three Key Considerations for Selecting the Right Visual to Tell Your Story

With so many visual options now at our fingertips, the challenge and opportunity for businesses is to choose the right visual to tell their story. Consider these first:

1. **Customer Preferences Reign Supreme**
   Know your customers. The more you understand your customers, the better you can serve them. In

selecting the right visuals to tell your story, factor in how and where—which devices and channels—your customers prefer to consume content.

Here are some important statistics:

- Four times as many consumers would prefer to watch a video about a product as to read about it[35]
- Using the word "video" in an e-mail subject line boosts open rates by 19 percent and click-through rates by 65 percent[36]
- 85 percent of Facebook videos are watched without sound[37]
- 51 percent of all video plays are on mobile devices[38]

By understanding how your customers prefer to consume content, you can factor in important design and distribution elements, driving further relevance with and interest from your target audience.

2. The Magic Is in the Visual Mix

It's easy to default to images or videos when shaping your visual storytelling strategy. While these mediums are fantastic and should compose a healthy portion of your visual storytelling efforts, do not discount the others. The format you select to tell your story depends on (a) the story and (b) the desired channel mix.

Alternatively, let's say your company is running a survey. Depending on your customer base, an infographic, a presentation, a white paper, an e-book, visuals with key stats, and maybe even expert quotes could all be logical ways to bring your story to life. Each of these elements works well across different platforms. You can share an infographic with a blog post, upload a presentation to SlideShare and LinkedIn, and post the quote and stat visuals on key social media channels with a link to the blog post or presentation. Taking these steps ensures a better, more cohesive customer experience.

Almost every time we speak at events about storytelling, someone always raises a hand and asks, "What percentage of my content strategy should be visual versus text based?" It ultimately comes down to how your target customer base prefers to consume information. In our experience, prioritizing visuals in the content you create is a winning formula. We recommend 75 to 90 percent of your content be visual-first. If it's a white paper or blog post, it should contain a number of supporting visuals to keep the customer's attention and make the content more memorable and shareable.

3. Change Is the Only Constant

The magic may be in the visual mix, but there is no set formula for the right blend of content. In fact, it's quite the opposite. As we covered in the Strategy Laws, it's important to build a strategic framework that allows you to continue to test and learn to ensure that you are generating the best results.

The always-on nature of digital and social media channels, coupled with ever-changing platforms and algorithms, has created an environment in which change is the only constant. In order to thrive in this climate, businesses need to analyze and measure the performance of their content on a regular basis to determine where to double down and optimize a win or assess if a strategic pivot is needed. Each piece of content offers an opportunity to connect with your customers, influencers, industry peers, and even the news media. As a result, it's critical to have that feedback loop of sentiment, top questions, or criticisms in place, allowing you to optimize or pivot as needed.

THE QUALITY LAW

One question marketers always ask us about crafting their content is, "What if we don't have the budget for an agency or freelancers to develop high-quality content?"

No worries. We say: the answer is in your pocket or your bag. We're talking about your mobile phone.

You shouldn't be afraid to go "low-fi." Create content on the go with your phone cameras. Phones have come a long way, and quality has improved significantly. When supplemented with the use of a photo editing app or video editing software, there's a lot of magic to be made, even on a miniscule budget.

We live in a world where people prefer real-time information over high-quality content that takes months to produce. Unless you are shooting a commercial, gone are the days when you have weeks or months to create pertinent content. As we will cover in the upcoming Urgency Law, relevance has a deadline. Live video is now preferred over the smartly planned in-studio video (with very few exceptions). Live shots—even blurry ones—get more engagement than carefully crafted brand banners.

Did you know that the phrase "Pics or it didn't happen" is now officially in the Urban Dictionary?

So don't sweat it if to capture a moment you might have to go "low-fi." That's fine. Your community will appreciate it. As you are looking at your metrics, you might just be surprised to see the low-fi pieces of content outperform the expensive ones. That's because "real" always trumps "manufactured."

A brand storytelling campaign that takes this sentiment to heart comes from Visit Faroe Islands. Frustrated by the lack of Google Street View for the islands, the tourism board decided to take matters into its own hands—and hooves—by attaching solar-powered 360-degree cameras to several of the islands' 80,000 sheep.

Yes, you read that correctly—360-degree cameras attached to sheep! Sounds crazy, right? Well, it's a brilliant example of how embracing your inner MacGyver can help solve your content creation woes.

If you're unsure of where the Faroe Islands are, you're not alone. The Faroe Islands are an archipelago of 18 mountainous islands located halfway between Iceland and Scotland in the North Atlantic Ocean. The archipelago's ruggedly beautiful terrain and remote location have made it an appealing, yet under-the-radar travel destination. That is, until Sheep View 360 made it an Internet sensation.

The Visit Faroe Islands team wanted to raise awareness of the islands' natural beauty to increase tourism, but lacked the resources to appropriately capture it. Plus, many of the most scenic parts of the islands were not accessible from the roads, but they were frequently traversed by the islands' sizeable population of freely wandering sheep. Visit Faroe Islands enlisted subject matter experts, including a shepherd and an inventor, to fashion a solar-powered 360-degree camera fit for even the most adventurous sheep. The camera takes a photo every minute and can also capture video.

The Sheep View 360 video footage is pretty amazing. The viewer is instantly transported on top of a sheep (which is often in motion!) and can take in the beautiful scenery as it roams. As it's a 360-degree experience, viewers can also control the direction of their view and see different angles. Watch it here: https://youtu.be/le_QEybrMMs. You may also see Sheep View 360 images from five different locations across the Faroe Islands on the appropriately named Sheepview Map. Just click on the sheep and you will be directed to Google Maps to see breathtaking images: https://visitfaroeislands.com/sheepview360/sheepview-map/.

Durita Dahl Andreassen, a project manager for Visit Faroe Islands, tells the story of the Sheep View 360 campaign. From sharing "her project" to get Google Street View's attention to video stories about "her sheep" on YouTube and the Visit Faroe Islands website, Durita became a friendly face and relatable ambassador for Visit Faroe Islands. Competitions to name some of the sheep and videos of locals campaigning to bring Google Street View to the islands further personalize their story and mission.[39]

Inspired by the global response and interest from local residents, the Visit Faroe Islands tourism board decided to loan 360-degree cameras to locals to capture their firsthand accounts of the best parts of the islands, which is how ship view, horse view, skateboard view, kayak view, and even wheelbarrow view came to be.[40]

The buzz around the campaign caught Google Street View's attention. Google called the initiative "brilliant," and sent its team to the Faroe Islands to capture additional imagery for Google Street View.

For a campaign that had a media budget of $0, it reached over two billion people, more than 4,000 times the number of residents of the Faroe Islands. Furthermore, two weeks into the campaign, hotels in Tórshavn were sold out, something not common at that time of year.[41]

All for having the imagination to strap 360-degree cameras onto sheep! So the next time you are frustrated by a lack of resources, budget, or fancy equipment, take a page from the Visit Faroe Islands playbook and embrace your inner MacGyver. How can you tell stories with the resources at your disposal?

The sooner you start thinking outside the box, the more you will push yourself and your colleagues to develop and test innovative ideas that could result in important breakthroughs for your company.

THE HUMOR LAW

If you love what you do, don't be afraid to have fun with it. Infusing your personality and humor into your marketing and customer engagement efforts will pay dividends.

There is obviously a time and a place for this approach; however, consider a few brands that don't take themselves seriously and reap humongous rewards such as Dollar Shave Club and Smart Car. We touched on the first earlier. Now let's take a look at the latter. This is one of our favorite examples of marketing done right. Smart Car shows just how to turn product criticism into an opportunity to have fun, drive engagement, *and* craftily highlight important product data.

Even though this example may be considered "aged" in the fast-moving world of social media, it never really gets old.

In June 2012 Clayton Hove, creative director at an ad agency in North Dakota and @adtothebone on Twitter, sent this tweet:

> Saw a bird had crapped on a Smart Car.
> Totaled it.

People thought it was hilarious and shared it with their friends.

What was Smart Car's inspired response?

> Couldn't have been one bird, @adtothebone.
> Sounds more like 4.5 million. Seriously, we did the math.

And truly they did. The company attached the infographic, which showed exactly how much bird crap it would take to damage a Smart Car's safety cell (specifically 4.5 million pigeon craps; 360,000 turkey craps; 45,000 emu craps). This got five times as many retweets as Clayton's original tweet, and it attracted a lot of media attention as well. What's more, it showed that the car manufacturer had a great sense of humor. Everybody loves to laugh. But what people loved more was the brand's confidence in its product, which this funny infographic showed very clearly. Including a variety of bird species was also a nice touch.[42]

Remember Tim Washer and the amazing work he's done with Cisco? Well, he has some words of advice for marketers keen to emulate Cisco's success with humorous promotional content:

- Start with your customer's pain point. Comedy comes from pain, so it's a rich area to mine. Focus on a problem that your company can solve. A great place to start is to explore the consequences of that problem not being solved, and exaggerate to the point of the ridiculous.
- Invent an absurd application for your product, as Cisco did with the ASR 9000 router in the Valentine's Day video.
- Add a funny sidekick. Have a company expert tell a story and have a sidekick toss in a few humorous responses to help you reach a different audience.
- Self-deprecating humor is a powerful way to humanize the brand. When a brand shows that it doesn't take itself too seriously, it demonstrates authenticity, as well as confidence.

Tim is right. Humor allows brands to connect with customers by showing their lighter side. Humor makes videos stand out, but the tone and content have to be appropriate to the brand's message, or audiences can wind up laughing at you rather than with you. Comedy videos can be used to great effect as part of wider marketing campaigns, especially as social media becomes ever more important to brands.

A word of caution: Always have checks and balances in place to ensure that what is funny to you might not be potentially offensive to someone else. You cannot always predict how people will react. However, having multiple internal stakeholders look at the creative and the message can help flag potential issues. Be diligent. Have fun with it, but make sure you get other perspectives.

THE URGENCY LAW

Being relevant equals being heard. But relevance has a deadline.

With the amount of online content increasing and the human attention span decreasing, it is harder than ever to be noticed as a brand. In the age of infobesity, real-time marketing is one of the strategies brand storytellers utilize to consistently stand out from the noise.

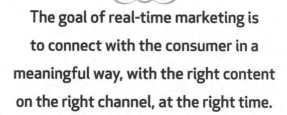

The goal of real-time marketing is to connect with the consumer in a meaningful way, with the right content on the right channel, at the right time.

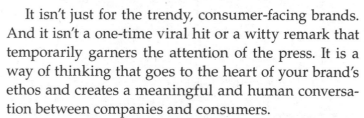

It isn't just for the trendy, consumer-facing brands. And it isn't a one-time viral hit or a witty remark that temporarily garners the attention of the press. It is a way of thinking that goes to the heart of your brand's ethos and creates a meaningful and human conversation between companies and consumers.

In the digital age the definition of great marketing has changed. It isn't a one-way brand broadcast. Great marketing and storytelling is now a conversation centered on communities and passions—and it needs to be flexible, responsive, and creative as never before.

In the past few years businesses started shifting their brand and content strategies to agile marketing in several ways:

- Investing in online listening tools that allow you to catch rising trends, hot conversations, and brand mentions early on
- Hiring people from the news industry, those with skill sets to create relevant content based on the immediate demands of consumers and do so in real time
- Adding always-on budgets that accommodate the need for on-the-spot creative brainstorming and execution
- Creating "brand storyteller" roles to address the shift from head marketing to heart marketing
- Putting processes in place that ensure immediate idea execution by involving the right stakeholders (strategy, creative, analytics, paid media, legal, community managers, etc.)
- Adopting the mantra "Customer care is the new marketing" and training customer service teams to focus on not only traditional support channels but online channels as well (social care)

This approach applies to different areas of customer experience management:

- Real-time content creation and creative optimization
- Campaign optimization
- Programmatic ad buying
- Social engagement
- Social customer care
- Product innovation

The effect of some of these areas, such as ad and campaign optimization, might not be publicly visible, but it drives huge business impact. The others, such as social engagement and customer care, are public and very visible. It is important to master each one.

Oftentimes when people think "real-time marketing," they think of it as capitalizing on a trend or event to get a quick brand hit. Think Arby's and Pharrell's Twitter exchange. Or NASA's clever and fully on-brand tweets during the 2014 Oscars. With the hashtag #RealGravity, NASA promoted itself using facts about gravity, a move that was obviously on-topic given that the movie *Gravity* was awarded seven Oscars that year. One of NASA's most popular tweets during the ceremony featured a gorgeous image of the earth accompanied by this text: "Congrats on another win at #Oscars2014 #Gravity for cinematography. Here's the #RealGravity—Earth from #ISS."

Even though leveraging a hot trend or a large event will get you the eyeballs, you might want to go for consistency and prioritize the "boring" over the "exciting." Consistently providing value to consumers through your real-time stories, content, and responses is more important than entertaining them with once-in-a-while hits. Put differently, engaging with your communities on a daily basis or helping your customers solve a problem will secure their loyalty more than a one-off fun tweet during a Super Bowl.

Very few brands do this "being responsive" thing well. Airlines are at the forefront of using social networks to help address real-time customer need. We both fly a lot, and we have gotten used to tweeting at airlines to help provide information or solve an issue. If you help customers in the moment, especially when time is of the essence, it means a million times more to them than when you tweet a funny meme.

Just recently I (Ekaterina) had "we are here to help you" exchanges with brands. One was with Tempur-Pedic: the company replied to my inquiry about its line of mattresses. Another was with K9 Ballistics, a manufacturer of chew-proof dog beds. Yes, they really are chew-proof. I swear by them. I have an adorable German Shepherd who is fond of chewing everything. I bought two beds from the company and have been very happy with them.

I was about to wash one of the dog beds when I had a moment of doubt about whether it could go in the washing machine, so I decided to check with the manufacturer. Sure, I could probably have found the answers online, but in a world where people are busier than ever, it gave me comfort to hear straight from the source without making any additional effort (Figure 4.2).

K9 Ballistics
@K9Ballistics

Following

Absolutely! All of our covers are machine-washable. Wash in cold water on a delicate cycle. Seal all Velcro or zipper closures before washing. Tumble dry on low heat or air dry.

Ekaterina Walter ⊘ @Ekaterina
Hey @K9Ballistics, is it okay to throw the bed stuffing in the washer (separately from the cover)?

9:37 PM - 26 Jan 2018

FIGURE 4.2   K9 Ballistics's reply to a customer inquiry

Quick and simple exchanges like this provide huge value and save a ton of time spent searching for answers online. The bonus? Customer loyalty and great word of mouth: I can't stop gushing about the product and the company!

Even if a brand's products are not suited to on-the-fly promotion or quick responses (for example, many companies in highly regulated industries must have input from the legal team before anything can be released), real-time marketing can still be used to monitor customer feedback and opinions, gauge customer involvement, or provide market research. If you think past the more headline-grabbing examples and look into how the data and analytics can work for you, you may find that there are many ways you can make use of the on-the-spot relevant insights they provide.

Obviously, real-time marketing gone wrong can lead to negative buzz. There have been some notable tweets and Facebook posts in response to events that have been in particularly bad taste. Kenneth Cole famously made a joke about the violent Cairo uprisings. And in 2017, Adidas, an official sponsor of the Boston Marathon, sent an e-mail to Boston Marathon finishers saying, "Congratulations, you survived the Boston Marathon!"[43] The response, as you can imagine, was far from positive.

The same goes for trying to insert real-time promotions into timely events. While in theory this makes sense, natural disasters and dangerous weather events should be avoided. Seems obvious, right? Well . . . American Apparel caught flack for trying to drive online sales during Hurricane Sandy, sending out an e-mail offering 20 percent off to customers in the New

England and Mid-Atlantic area impacted by the storm over a 36-hour time window, saying, "In case you're bored during the storm."[44]

Real-time marketing can show your brand's responsiveness to current events and situations, but be careful. Always assess how real-time content aligns with your brand and fits into your wider marketing objectives, and how your community might respond.

6 Ps of Real-Time Marketing Done Right

When thinking about executing your real-time strategy, consider the 6 Ps Framework™. It will guide you through the key priorities and elements you will need to execute it successfully.

People

First, understand what skill sets you are missing (content strategy, community management, writing, analytics, etc.) and ensure that the team has the right people. Second, build a list of stakeholders (such as PR, legal, etc.) who need to be involved for effective always-on content and engagement strategies.

Process

Develop and perfect the process that will ensure smooth execution when story-making opportunities present themselves. Remember, what works for one industry might not work for another. Similarly, what works for one geography might not work for another. Always customize and adjust as necessary. Don't allow your process to be rigid and inflexible. That can be the death of your real-time strategy.

Preparation

Preparation and planning are not the same thing. Preparation means spending time, effort, and resources on ensuring your response is polished and agile.

Oreo had a number of big real-time brand story-telling hits, starting with the famous "You can still dunk in the dark" tweet. During the 2013 Super Bowl, the power went out in the Superdome during the showdown between the San Francisco 49ers and the Baltimore Ravens. Oreo seized on the opportunity, and tweeted this during the 34-minute hiatus: "Power out? No problem." The tweet was accompanied by the image of an Oreo cookie with the message "You can still dunk in the dark." The brand made history and put real-time marketing on the map.

Since then many brands have tried to emulate Oreo's success. Often quite unsuccessfully. Why? Because it wasn't a "happy accident," and therefore can't be easily replicated by releasing a single image or witty response. Oreo had spent months building up its real-time marketing memory muscle using agile marketing techniques, including the 100-day #DailyTwist campaign, for which the company created daily visuals starring the Oreo cookie, inspired by pop culture, milestones, or the news of the day, in celebration of its 100th birthday in 2012. So when the now famous Super Bowl moment happened, it had the right people and processes in place to get both the creative done and immediate approvals secured in real time, literally.

Planning

Planning means you are ready for big events such as Christmas, the Super Bowl, or the Oscars. This allows you to plan for participation in those discussions online. Again, be careful not to interrupt the conversation with a forced message. Only jump in when it makes sense thematically and aligns with your brand message. NASA knew there was a good chance the movie *Gravity* would be nominated for the 2014 Oscars, and it planned for it.

Planning also means having the right infrastructure in place to be able to spot and respond to the right people, at the right time, on the right channel. And, as we mentioned earlier, you must have always-on budgets allocated for just such scenarios.

Practice

To get really good at agile marketing, you have to practice it. Oreo practiced and got really good at it. The real-time response needs to be ingrained in the everyday running of a brand's marketing. Practice will ensure that when that big opportunity comes along, you will be poised and ready to respond in an original, well-thought-out, and creative way.

Playbook

Your last step should be creating a blueprint of the approach you've seen the most success with (Figure 4.3). Use it for future campaigns, and share it across the organization (business units, geographies, functional teams).

To be a successful real-time storyteller in the digital age of personalization, your brand should adopt an always-on attitude. Many brands have set up social media command centers to monitor the social sphere and engage with their communities. Having an always-on attitude can bring limitless rewards when you capitalize on the multitude of storytelling opportunities.

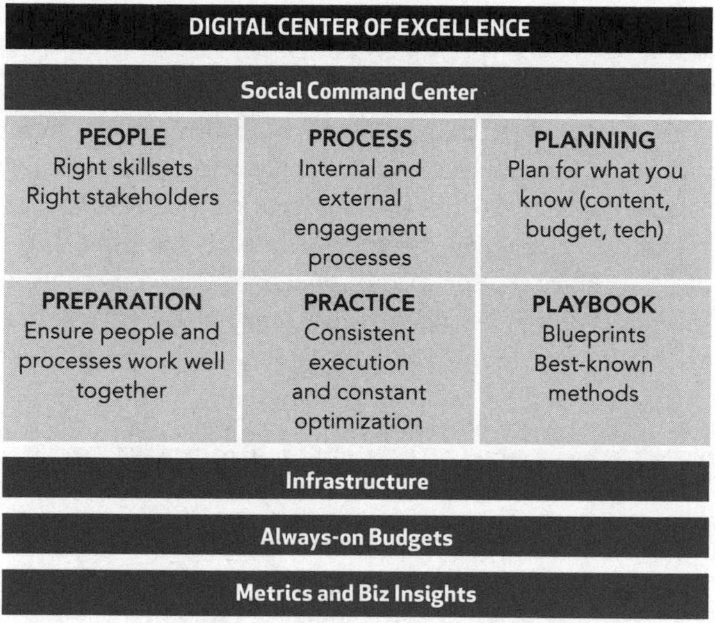

DIGITAL CENTER OF EXCELLENCE		
Social Command Center		
PEOPLE Right skillsets Right stakeholders	**PROCESS** Internal and external engagement processes	**PLANNING** Plan for what you know (content, budget, tech)
PREPARATION Ensure people and processes work well together	**PRACTICE** Consistent execution and constant optimization	**PLAYBOOK** Blueprints Best-known methods
Infrastructure		
Always-on Budgets		
Metrics and Biz Insights		

FIGURE 4.3 How the 6Ps Framework™ fits within your Digital Center of Excellence

Just like the laundry detergent company Tide did when it was quick to react to the footage of its product being used by NASCAR crews to clean up a spill after a Daytona 500 crash. That fast response helped its resulting video commercial go viral. The video showed the footage of the crash with the Fox TV commentators in the background noting the "bizarre twist to Daytona 500" and a "new use for the laundry detergent." Tide smartly overlaid the following text across the 16-second spot: "You keep inventing stains. We'll keep inventing ways to get them out. #tidepower" The spot closed with the commentators saying: "Whatever it takes."

Whatever it takes indeed.

This 6 Ps approach can be applied to a variety of business and marketing strategies.

With the right attitude, the right systems in place, and plenty of preparation and planning, more companies can make the most of real-time opportunities to tell stories relevant to their brand. The results are greater audience engagement, more responsive customer service, better brand awareness, and increased sales. It is all about finding and creating the stories that are right for you and your customers.

THE UTILITY LAW

There is a new phenomenon sweeping the world of marketing: utilitarian marketing—providing would-be customers with something useful while also delivering your marketing message.

Utilitarian marketing provides a valuable service to customers, whether they spend money with the company or not. It is a truly selfless look at what people might need and taking an action to help make their lives better.

In the age of infobesity, companies are struggling to separate themselves from the digital noise and to draw meaningful attention and interest from their current and potential customers.

This struggle happens mainly because internally there is a big tug-of-war going on between marketers' desire to plaster their product-centric messaging across all of their assets (after all, they need to justify that annual budget, right?) and their desire to create something truly amazing, something that will be used by customers time and again, gently reminding them about the brand that helped create that fantastic experience.

Which approach is better?

Chances are, as a customer, you are thinking the latter. But the problem for companies is that the latter means either putting the brand second to the customer experience or, heaven help us, removing any reference to your product, service, or brand altogether. Therein lies the dilemma.

According to Localytics, one in four mobile applications are never used again after being downloaded, and 80 percent of all app users churn within 90 days.[45]

That's not the case, however, with the SitorSquat Restroom Finder app created by Charmin back in 2009. The popular travel app helps people find clean public restrooms based on user-generated ratings and reviews. All you have to do is type in your location and the app shows you a map with restroom options: the ones featuring green toilet paper rolls are sit-worthy, red paper rolls are a squat, and gray rolls mean there isn't sufficient data to make the determination.

The app allows users to rate restrooms and upload photos to help others identify the best restroom stops to make. As app use increases and the public contributes, the app gets better with increased participation. More than 100,000 restrooms have been added by consumers, and Charmin keeps improving its user interface and adding new features. Using the app, which has been praised in multiple publications, keeps Charmin top of mind. In addition to providing customers with a valuable resource, Charmin can leverage app data such as user-generated content, ratings, and reviews to craft micro stories about its brand. Who says utility doesn't pay off?

The Nationwide mobile app is another example of great utility. It's a useful step-by-step application that walks people through everything they need to know if they have just been in a car accident: from collecting accident information to taking pictures of the damaged vehicle and recording the location where the accident happened. The app has a flashlight built in (for night-time accidents), helps initiate and expedite claims, and locates towing services. You can even let company representatives know the best time for them to follow up with you. While Nationwide creates content and tips on these topics, taking it a step further to truly add value in an easy-to-use way is what truly differentiates it from others in the space.

Let's go beyond apps and look at several brands that strike the right balance between utility and marketing.

The University of Engineering and Technology of Peru wanted to inspire young people to pursue careers in engineering and did this in a powerful way—by showcasing how technology can help solve local problems. One of those problems is the lack of running water in the city of Lima. The humidity in the city runs incredibly high, at 98 percent. So the university had the brilliant idea to develop the world's first water-producing billboard that created drinking water out of thin air. Engineers leveraged built-in reverse osmosis technology that captured water vapor and turned it into water while purifying it. The billboard produced 9,540 liters of water in just three months, helping hundreds of families and inspiring the next generation of engineers to study at the university.[46]

Another great example is Samsung's mobile phone charging stations that you see across all major airports. It's one of those ideas that is so blindingly obvious that once you've seen it you wonder why no one had thought of it before. What do travelers need to do at airports? Charge their phones. Cue Samsung's phone charging hubs that allow passengers to charge their phones while they're waiting and put Samsung's name in large letters right before their eyes. Not only does it help raise Samsung's profile, it also provides a hugely useful service to airport users. We are both avid travelers, so we can tell you from personal experience that this is one of the coolest things a brand has done to help people. Exaggeration? We don't think so. Have you ever walked throughout an airport desperately trying to find an electric outlet? No? We have. It's the stuff of nightmares!

If these examples have taught you anything, it's that people are looking for utility—something that will help make their lives easier, solve problems, and add value. Look closely and you'll notice a theme: each customer-centric solution also opens the door for brand storytelling. From uncovering the best public toilets, to taking the guesswork out of a difficult situation (a car accident), and providing your local community with clean drinking water, each company or institution launched these offerings for a reason: to serve their customers or their community, but also to fulfill each organization's mission and purpose, further validating their necessity. These offerings may not show management immediate benefits or attractive numbers, but the inspiration, value, and positive impact on their current and prospective customer base will no doubt pay long-term dividends.

Utilitarian marketing, when done correctly, does more than just provide a valuable service to customers: it powers remarkable customer experiences. Which is critical if you take into consideration the research we shared from Gartner highlighting how 89 percent of companies now compete primarily on customer experience.[47]

Also, have you thought about the halo effect great customer experiences provide? Remarkable customer experiences travel far beyond the initial customer. When customers have an incredible experience with your brand, they are 77 percent more likely to recommend your company, products, or services to others.[48] That's where the magic happens. When customers recommend and share their stories about your company, they will be told and retold by their network, resulting in a snowball effect about how amazing you are. Who wouldn't want that?

This is why the "sell more by selling less" principle should become every company's marketing mantra. You can't always expect to produce a viral hit or a great marketing campaign, but what you can count on is your ability to find customers' pain points and do everything you can to help them find solutions, make their lives easier, and add value either through content, applications, or real-time social responses.

So stop promoting, and start informing and helping. And do it authentically.

How?

- Think about what your customers really need
- Stay true to your brand's core messages
- Put the service first—and the marketing second
- Aim for loyalty, not sales
- Think longer-term rather than instant ROI
- Put your resources behind inspiring advocacy and nurturing positive word of mouth rather than creating short-term one-off marketing campaigns

Utilitarian marketing is all about heart. That's why brands find it so hard to execute. The first reaction from marketers usually is: "How can we get our marketing message out on this?" But building loyalty is a long-term game, and caring about others has to come before caring about sales. You've got to remember that through advocacy, loyalty, and authentic engagement, you will build the sort of super-customers whose brand devotion will last long after traditional marketing campaigns have been forgotten.

THE OWNERSHIP LAW

A picture is worth a thousand words, right? Nope. More like $2.2 billion.

That's exactly what a California woman wants Chipotle Mexican Grill to pay her for using a picture of her in their marketing without her permission. Leah Caldwell filed suit in the U.S. District Court of Colorado on December 27, 2016, alleging Chipotle used her image without her consent for commercial gain. She claims that the image was taken without her knowledge, and when approached by the photographer, she refused to sign a release form. Moreover, the image was later altered to add beer bottles, which associated her with drinking alcohol, a fact she didn't appreciate either. The picture was taken in 2006. She was shocked when in 2014 she found it in an Orlando restaurant and then later in several California locations. If you are wondering about the $2.2 billion number, it amounts to the company's profits over a nine-year period.[49]

We may live in the digital age when pictures are being snapped every second and are freely shared across social channels, but that doesn't mean the rules of ethical marketing practices have changed.

Just as you own the rights to your branded content, consumers own the rights to the content they produce. Just because they feature your products or your brand doesn't mean you can automatically reuse them in your stories or on your channels.

If you are aggregating content from various social channels, then you should follow a strict set of rules and guidelines for redisplaying that content. It includes credit, links, dates, cited sources, disclosures, and other criteria. If you are reusing images or videos in promoting your product or your brand, you must have written permission from the creator of the content. Utilizing user-generated content such as customer stories, images, videos, and original creative assets always requires their permission. Without exception!

Years ago, when I (Ekaterina) was beginning to build social communities for Intel, I noticed that a lot of die-hard fans were producing amazing images and videos to celebrate the Intel brand in unique ways. So I decided to create a board on Pinterest called Fan Love to celebrate their creativity. To be able to feature the images, I reached out to each fan individually, asking them for permission, which they gladly gave.

That approach, however, is not scalable. When embarking on larger and more involved user-generated content (UGC) campaigns, make sure you use a vendor or a technology that has the governance guardrails built in. It saves you time and makes it easier for your team to run the campaign. Most important, it ensures that you own any content produced by the participants, with their consent.

There are a number of other scenarios you should consider. For example, when working with a celebrity (even for voice-over work) or using someone's music, remember that there is always a shelf life for how long you can use the assets. At the end of that time, you should cease using the content just like your contract states. This goes for your affiliates, franchisees, geographies, and partners. There are technologies that allow you to control the use of those assets on a global scale and ensure you are not stuck with large fines when the rules are not followed.

This is just one example. There are many others. We won't list them all here. It is our intention, however, to caution you and suggest you work closely with your legal and compliance departments to ensure you are very clear on the rules associated with every possible scenario.

THE BRAND PROTECTION LAW

As a marketer, it is your responsibility to try to protect the brand in everything you do. And by that we don't mean fall back on fear. Fear won't lead to innovation. Just the opposite. That said, there needs to be a healthy balance of risk-taking and common sense.

Disclosures

Did you know that the Instagram influencer marketing space alone is worth over $1 billion? And according to Mediakix, the company that published this statistic, by 2019 the market will have grown to a whopping 2.38 billion dollars.[50] However, 93 percent of influencers are not meeting FTC regulations with their posts.[51] This could result in lawsuits and big fines for brands and influencers alike if they don't follow FTC disclosure guidelines.

Since 2009, Sony, Xbox, Cole Haan, Lord & Taylor, and other brands have been penalized by the FTC for not properly disclosing that messages shared by influencers were paid messages.

Warner Bros. got into hot water when it paid YouTube influencers with large followings for favorable reviews, but failed to disclose that. Here's the statement issued by the FTC on July 11, 2016: "Warner Bros. Home Entertainment, Inc. has settled Federal Trade Commission charges that it deceived consumers during a marketing campaign for the video game Middle Earth: Shadow of Mordor, by failing to adequately disclose that it paid online 'influencers,' including the wildly popular 'PewDiePie,' thousands of dollars to post positive gameplay videos on YouTube and social media. Over the course of the campaign, the sponsored videos were viewed more than 5.5 million times."[52]

Even though Warner Bros. wasn't hit by a financial penalty, the company was barred from conducting similar ad campaigns in the future.

It doesn't stop with brands, either. In 2017 the FTC sent letters to 90 influencers reminding them of the need to properly disclose their relationships with brands in their social postings. The FTC then published an article appropriately titled "Influencers, are your #materialconnection #disclosures #clearandconspicuous?"[53]

Finding the coolest ways to tell our stories doesn't mean that we ignore our legal and ethical responsibilities as brands. You need to be intimately familiar with the Federal Trade Commission (FTC) endorsement guides. You can find them here: https://www.ftc.gov/tips-advice/business-center/guidance/ftcs-endorsement-guides-what-people-are-asking. Moreover, if you work with influencers, don't expect them to shoulder the responsibility. Make sure they follow the guidelines to a tee. After all, *your* brand will be under attack if something goes wrong. Always assume that the burden is on you as the brand and clearly communicate to influencers how, what, and where the required disclosures should go.

This advice goes beyond celebrity and influencer endorsements and applies to promotions, contests, and sweepstakes.

><><

Any form of paid endorsement by *anyone* on *any* social channel, *regardless of* the size of someone's following, needs to be done according to proper disclosure rules. No exceptions.

><><

Don't Be That Brand

Too often we see brands outrage customers through campaigns, content, imagery, and videos deemed racist or offensive toward people's race, color, gender, sexual orientation, nationality, religion, or political views.

In January 2018 the retailer H&M was forced to apologize for an ad showing a young African American boy wearing a hoodie that read "coolest monkey in the jungle." The sweatshirt sparked outrage on social media because it referred to an insensitive racial slur.

"We sincerely apologize for this image," H&M said in an e-mail sent to CBS MoneyWatch. "It has now been removed from all online channels, and the product will not be for sale in the United States. We believe in diversity and inclusion in all that we do, and will be reviewing our internal routines."[54]

Another retailer, The Children's Place, found itself in the middle of controversy by selling a T-shirt that reinforced stereotypes that girls are not interested in math. The T-shirt showed a checklist of "my best subjects," with shopping, music, and dancing checked while math remained unchecked.[55] #JustWOW.

Let's linger on the latter example for a moment, shall we? We get the idea behind gendered marketing. For some of the products that are specifically targeted at either men or women, it might make sense. However, in most cases, it's just inappropriate. Like the Bic for Her pen for women, because apparently our delicate female hands can't handle a regular pen. We need a she-pen. Thank heaven for the color pink, too. That saves us all from confusion.

Our "favorite," however, is Lady Doritos. This one takes the first, second, and third prizes in the gendered-marketing-gone-wrong category.

It all started on January 31, 2018, when during an interview with Indra Nooyi, CEO of PepsiCo, on the "Freakonomics Radio" podcast, she said that women eat Doritos differently than men.

"They don't like to crunch too loudly in public," she said. "And they don't lick their fingers generously, and they don't like to pour the little broken pieces and the flavor into their mouth."[56]

OK, let's just pause for a second: a female CEO said that!

When asked if PepsiCo (which owns Frito-Lay, the company that manufactures Doritos) was working on creating a female version of chips, she answered: "It's not a male and female as much as, 'Are there snacks for women that can be designed and packaged differently?' And yes, we are looking at it, and we're getting ready to launch a bunch of them soon. For women, low-crunch, the full taste profile, not having so much of the flavor stick on the fingers, and how can you put it in a purse? Because women love to carry a snack in their purse."

It blew up from there. A storm of comedy and outrage on social media. International press coverage.

A while later the company issued the following statement: "The reporting on a specific Doritos product for female consumers is inaccurate. We already have Doritos for women—they're called Doritos, and they're enjoyed by millions of people every day. At the same time, we know needs and preferences continue to evolve, and we're always looking for new ways to engage and delight our consumers."[57]

Some argue that the announcement came a bit too late. The data from Digimind, which tracks consumer sentiment, suggests that the Doritos brand has taken a significant perception hit. Digimind's team was tracking sentiment around Doritos for the Super Bowl and discovered that between game day and several days later when the "Lady Doritos" news exploded, the negative opinions about the brand spiked 138 percent.[58]

There were so many brilliant responses to the news. Here are some select tweets for you (you are welcome!):

@thistallawkgirl:

Women: We want equal pay for equal work and an end to sex discrimination in the workplace.

Society: Here's a bag of Lady Doritos so you won't have to crunch too loudly in front of your male colleagues.

@bairdjulia:

WE DO NOT WANT: #LadyDoritos

Lady Laxatives

Lady Power Tools

Lady Shavers

Little Lady Lego

Lady Wages

WE DO WANT:

Lady Prime Minister

Lady Leaders

Lady Pope

@everywhereist: What if Lady Doritos are just regular Doritos but when a woman buys a bag she only gets 77% of the chips a guy would. #LadyDoritos

@faithchoyce: To compete with Lady Doritos, Lays has designed a new chip especially for men: It requires them to understand enthusiastic consent before they can open the bag.

And then there was an unparalleled video response by Rhett and Link, creators and hosts of Good Mythical Morning. It was appropriately titled "Eat Like a Lady" and was viewed over two million times in the first week after posting. It's truly a masterpiece. Go ahead and watch it: https://www.facebook.com/RhettAndLink /videos/10155445594701476/. No, really. Watch it. We'll wait. The last two seconds are priceless, aren't they?

Whether it's a new product line or a marketing asset, you have to have a system in place that ensures a diverse set of opinions before you go public with it. For products, engage select user groups or do some market testing before you proceed with an idea. For marketing assets, have a system of checks and balances that allows multiple stakeholders to assess the potential risk of a creative or a message.

I (Ekaterina) have worked with a number of brands that have created millennial advisory groups or included the members of the Diversity team on the stakeholder list for major creative campaigns to ensure that nothing gets lost in the translation of an idea into a marketing asset. This approach is especially important when you outsource the work to a vendor or an agency because you have no visibility into its inner workings. In this case, not only should you refer to the Authenticity Playbook yourself, you should ensure your agency partners are intimately familiar with it.

THE OPTIMIZATION LAW

As we have shown in this chapter, there are many elements and key considerations that go into crafting your story. And if you're anything like us, you absolutely love the creative and strategic process. But here's the thing: bringing amazing stories to life will only take you so far. If you want to ensure that your stories have strong reach, engagement, and relevance, make sure you prioritize their optimization. Test, measure, learn, optimize, repeat (Figure 4.4).

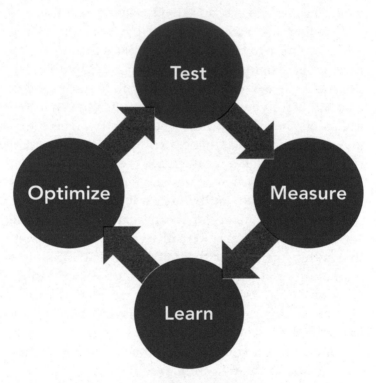

FIGURE 4.4   Storytelling optimization approach

Just as your stories were crafted with specific key messages and audiences in mind, the way you optimize them across paid, owned, and earned media

(POEM) ensures that they reach the right person at the right moment on the right channel. However, the types of media are not the only elements that you should optimize. Everything that forms your story, from your key messages to your call to action, visual mediums, size/length, and more, can provide learning opportunities that further unlock optimization for brand storytelling success.

Optimize:

- Ad format
- Ad targeting
- Call to action
- Channel mix (POEM)
- Content mix
- Copy
- Design style
- Key messages
- Linkable content (e.g., landing page, website, blog, news article)
- Storyline
- Timing/frequency
- Size (images) and/or length (video)
- Tone of voice
- Visual media

Think of the many elements of your story like pieces of a puzzle. As you create and distribute your stories, evaluate each element in real time to understand what appeals and resonates the most with your target audience.

You may be thinking, "But wait, I've already obsessed over all of the elements that go into creating and bringing this story to life. I'll just see how it performs and then factor those results into my next storytelling campaign."

While you could certainly take this approach, you would be selling yourself short. If you take inspiration from one thing, it's that great storytellers play to their audience. If each element of your story is a different piece of the puzzle, consider your audience the wise voice teaching you how to fit them together. Sure, you could choose not to listen and do it your own way, but why would you? Today the leaders across every industry are the ones who are the most agile in how they pivot and optimize based on strategic intelligence from real-time customer feedback, major industry changes, competitor insights, and more.

A compelling case for optimization comes from Coca-Cola. When Coca-Cola relaunched its corporate website as a digital magazine, customer feedback and site traffic shaped its content strategy. To determine the optimal content mix for its digital magazine, Coca-Cola decided to treat every day like it was Election Day. And no, it was not electing new leaders. It was "electing" stories and content strategies based on their level of engagement. In year one, Coca-Cola made more than 60 real-time tweaks to the site, all based on customer feedback. By continually testing and learning from the popularity and engagement around different types of articles and stories, the company experienced surprising wins and shocking losses. It turns out, some of the content that Coca-Cola's team thought would be top performers fell completely flat, while others totally surprised them with their success. As a result of extensive testing and optimization, Coca-Cola's Unbottled blog secured a 106 percent increase in page views, while its home page saw a 1,247 percent increase in visits, proving to the company that the company's "Every Day Is Election Day" strategy was a powerful game-changer.[59]

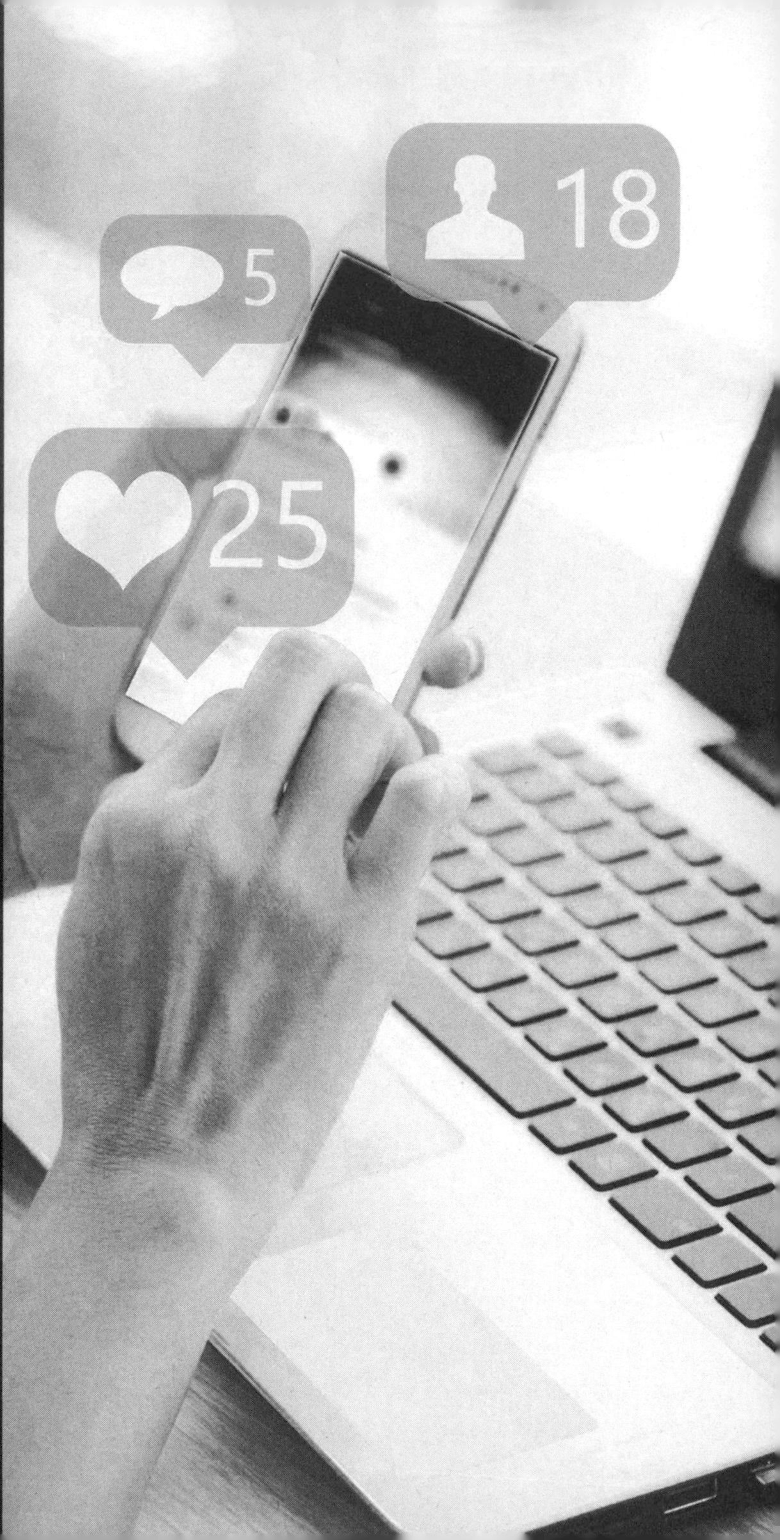
18
5
25

Chapter **5**

THE CHANNEL LAWS

SHARE YOUR STORY

In 2015, the United Kingdom was abuzz with the solar eclipse; the country had not seen one in 16 years. While many brands rose to the occasion with their eclipse-inspired campaigns, one brand stood out.

Why? Because it eclipsed the sun with its brand—literally. As in, *The Sun* newspaper.

The brand behind this brilliant stunt was Oreo. Oreo partnered with *The Sun* in the United Kingdom to "eclipse the *Sun*," with the paper's first-ever translucent cover wrap, which featured the iconic cookie and a black translucent "sky" eclipsing the paper's cover on the next page. Inside the paper, two additional translucent Oreo ads were also featured, further tying the beloved cookie to the solar eclipse.

But, it didn't stop there. Building off a successful print activation, the company also turned to out-of-home with digital billboards in London and Edinburgh, including the iconic one in Piccadilly Circus in London, the equivalent to Times Square in New York City. On the billboards, viewers could watch as the Oreo cookie followed the moon's movements to eclipse the sun, per real-time data from the Royal Astronomical Society.

To further drive conversation as the eclipse was happening, Oreo also purchased the promoted trend #OreoEclipse on Twitter and drove additional sharing through brand generated tweets with clever eclipse-themed visuals. With the weather doing its best to spoil the eclipse with grey skies, Oreo's ability to capture and film the actual eclipse, plus its branded recreation, resulted in a mix of useful and entertaining content for its customer base to savor the event—ideally with an Oreo cookie, of course!

In total, the #OreoEclipse campaign reached 20 million people in just one day across its integrated channel mix.[1] The goal of the campaign was to raise awareness with UK consumers who typically buy biscuits to be consumed with tea or as a snack, but pursue other options. By cleverly activating around the solar eclipse with an integrated yet personalized campaign across print, out-of-home, online, and social media, Oreo successfully achieved its goals. Sales of Oreo cookies rose 59 percent in the United Kingdom the week following the #OreoEclipse, with the month of the eclipse, March, breaking sales records for the company.[2]

While the right visual or narrative may bring your story to life, it's the channel that gives your stories a home. And here's the exciting thing: each channel brings something different to the table. Whether it's print, out-of-home billboards, online communities, product packaging, social media, or something else, each has its own spoken and unspoken rules of engagement. To connect successfully with various communities, you need to know and consider not only your channel mix, but the rules and best practices of each channel as part of your overall strategy and approach.

THE PERSONALIZATION LAW

As Oreo's campaign showcases, it's incredibly important to understand the unique features of each channel so you can personalize your brand story accordingly. Gone are the days when it was acceptable to spray the same piece of content across multiple platforms. Instead, today's brand storytelling leaders are embracing the special features of each channel to provide personalized experiences.

Case in point: who could have predicted how amazing it would be to turn your head into a giant taco, courtesy of Taco Bell's Cinco de Mayo Snapchat Sponsored Lens? While we're sure Taco Bell had an inkling, how could it have predicted that its playful taco head would garner 224 million views in one day?[3]

Or when Uruguay-based agency The Electric Factory Group tapped the power of out-of-home digital billboards to present poster-sized, bacteria-filled petri dishes to raise awareness about hygiene. Installed in shopping centers and malls in Uruguay, the oversized digital petri dishes illustrated the shocking number of germs found on everyday items like our mobile phones, money, or video game controllers. Seen by more than one million people, the goal was to gross people out enough to encourage them to wash their hands more. The secondary goal, however, was for the agency to prove to its clients that out-of-home can still make an impact—with the right message and the right creative. Suffice it to say, it worked because the choice of channel and the powerful message made it hard to ignore.[4]

Anyone else feel like washing their hands now?

Nowadays companies have more channels than ever to tell their story on, presenting both a challenge and an opportunity. While we acknowledge that delivering personalized, relevant experiences across all customer touchpoints is no easy feat, the missed opportunity cost presents a powerful rationale for investment.

According to Accenture's 2017 study on hyperrelevant customer experiences, 4 out of 10 consumers switched companies because of poor personalization, costing companies an estimated $756 billion in just one year.[5]

Accenture's study also reveals a powerful upside, revealing that 75 percent of consumers are more likely to buy from a brand when they're recognized, remembered, or served with relevant recommendations.[6]

For companies that are concerned about coming across as Big Brother and being too eerily personal with their customers, fret not. Accenture Interactive's research on personalization indicates that 80 percent of customers report they've never received a communication that was too personal or invasive. Of the 20 percent who have, the reason for half of the respondents was focused around third-party data as opposed to data the customers had provided.[7]

With personalization, the best tip we can offer is to put yourself in your customers' shoes. How would you feel if a company knew you were pregnant before you told your significant other or family members? Target got itself in hot water for this very reason. In 2012, the company's data analysis wizardry successfully predicted that a teenage girl was pregnant before she told her family. Based on her purchase data, the company sent coupons to her house for products that a woman who was expecting would typically appreciate. In this case, not only did the girl not appreciate it, her father got really mad and called Target out. The company realized that it had crossed the line—and creeped people out—prompting it to take a step back and curate a mix of offers across departments.[8]

The best practice is to factor the customer experience into the personalized experiences you deliver. Even if you have robust purchase data or can employ hypertargeting tactics like social media ads, the most successful efforts and stories are those that deliver a value or benefit to your customers—without crossing ethical lines.

The same personalization principle also applies to business functions. Customer service is a prime example of a business function that is often overlooked, yet adds incredible value, especially when personalized across channels. Aspect's 2017 Customer Experience Study revealed that:

- 68 percent of customers gave more business to companies that provided good customer service[9]
- 67 percent of consumers believe that a personalized customer service experience is more important than the speed of service[10]
- 48 percent of consumers feel the ability to interact in the method or manner of their choice is the most important facet of a personalized customer experience—three times more important than knowing their name/history[11]

Choosing the right channel is critical in any function, whether it's marketing, sales, or support. Speaking about the latter, for example, research from CEB Global found that asking consumers to switch from their preferred support channel can actually decrease loyalty by 10 percent.[12] In Aspect's 2017 Customer Experience Study, the company puts the power of channel-specific customer service into perspective with "The Toilet Index." Oh yes, you read that correctly! Before you "poo-poo" it as a gimmick, hear us out. The company asked survey respondents to rate if they would rather clean a toilet or contact customer service via a range of channels. The Toilet Index uncovered that IVR, or interactive voice response, frustrated customers the most, so much so that 39 percent of customers would rather clean a toilet than seek help from an IVR system.[13] When it comes to other sources, the number drops to 35 percent for social media, 18 percent for text, 14 percent for e-mail, 13 percent for voice, and 11 percent for in-person support.[14]

The key takeaway here is that different segments of your customers will have different needs and preferred channels of communication. At a time when companies compete almost entirely on customer experience, those that can add value through personalization will emerge as the leaders in their industries. The key is to put yourself in your customers' shoes and understand what types of experiences they want personalized per channel. From content and stories, to customer service and even ads, the more you know your customers, the more you can deliver personalized experiences. But remember, with great knowledge comes great power. And with great power comes great responsibility. Add value, but don't cross the line!

THE CHANNEL MIX LAW

While each channel brings something different to the table, as you saw with the #OreoEclipse campaign, how you curate your story across multiple channels can be an important differentiator when it comes to reach, engagement, and perception. Today's consumers have more channels at their fingertips than ever before, and they prioritize those that deliver the greatest value to them. However, even with prioritization, companies are rarely in a situation where consumers see their content on only one channel. Quite the opposite, actually! The average social media user has accounts on five different channels—and that's before you take into account the other online and offline touchpoints with your company.[15]

As a result, you need to consider what the right channel mix is for your business and for your customers. Additionally, you should ensure that the personalized experiences by channel form a cohesive experience for consumers who see your stories across multiple channels.

Right Channel, Right Context, Right Format

Before we explore the channel mix, let's first discuss the key considerations you need to keep in mind while outlining your channel strategy:

1. **Prioritize Your Channel Mix**

   We are not advocating that your company needs to be present on every channel. Even for the largest companies out there, it's a daunting prospect to deliver meaningful customer experiences at scale across all channels. Instead, prioritize those where your customers are, with one important caveat: make it clear to your customers where you are present! List the channels you are committed to on your website. Bonus points if you can also specify the response time across specific channels. By showing the current wait time for a customer to reach you on the phone, via e-mail, or across specific social media channels, you are not only managing customer expectations, but also providing a better experience.

2. Don't Invest Only in Rented Land

While it's tempting to go big on social media channels, a word of caution: they are rented land. Just like you would diversify an investment portfolio, you need to diversify your channel mix across the channels you own and those you don't. Owned channels are the ones your company is in charge of: website, blog, packaging, in-store experience, and more. With the channels you don't own, you need to navigate factors like algorithm changes or the fact that social networks could shut down with little warning. Don't put all your eggs in one basket—especially if you don't own the basket.

3. Shiny Object Syndrome Will Only Take You So Far

Beware of experts who are fond of making sweeping statements like, "traditional is dead" or "blogs are dead." The current business environment makes it easy to fixate on the shiny objects of the moment and lose focus on the bigger picture. At the end of the day, each channel has its use and value. Of course, some channels will be of more value to some businesses than others based on the makeup of their customer base. Do your own due diligence as it pertains to the channels that matter to you and your customers.

4. Champion the Spoken and Unspoken Rules of Each Channel

Whatever channels you choose to be present on, personalize and follow the spoken and unspoken rules of each. Spoken rules are the parameters set by the channel to guide the content you share and how you engage with your community. For example, on Twitter, a spoken rule is the 280-character limit. Alternately, on Tumblr, an unspoken rule is that GIFs are the best approach. Using GIFs is not a rule or a necessity, but it's what the community wants. The same could be said for hashtags on Instagram; they're not required, but it is an unspoken rule that using them makes your content more discoverable.

More Channels, More Opportunities

Just like the magic is in the visual and content mix, it's also in your channel mix and how you bring different stories to life through them.

As we have already gone into depth on various social media channels throughout the book, we're going to use this chapter as an opportunity to expand on brand storytelling best practices across several traditional and digital channels.

Here is a comprehensive list of traditional, digital, and social media channels to spark your creativity:

- Ads
- Blogs
- Chatbots
- Customer communities

- Digital magazines
- E-mail
- Events
- In-store signage
- Mobile apps
- News outlets
- Podcasts
- Product
- Print
- SMS/text
- Social media channels (Twitter, Instagram, Snapchat, YouTube, etc.)
- TV/film product placements
- Voice/audio skills
- Virtual assistants
- Website

Let's explore some of them.

Ads

In a time when customer experience is paramount, advertising can feel like a double-edged sword. From TV, to radio, out-of-home billboards, print, digital, and social media, marketers are constantly in pursuit of the elusive "right customer, right message, right channel, right moment." Layer in the sophistication of ad targeting solutions, coupled with the pay-to-play environment of most traditional, digital, and social media channels, and it's easy to see why most companies still invest heavily in advertising. According to Statista, in 2017, global advertising spend totaled just over $591 billion, a 17 percent increase from $488.48 billion in 2014.[16] By 2020, Statista predicts that global advertising spend will hit just over $724 billion.[17]

Despite advertising's continued growth, the vast majority of customers still perceive it to be impersonal and too sales-y. Research from HubSpot shows that 91 percent of people say ads are more intrusive today than two years ago.[18] Furthermore, specific ad formats can even create a negative customer experience, with four out of five people reporting that they have left a webpage because of a pop-up or autoplaying video ad.[19]

However, not all hope is lost for advertisers. HubSpot's research highlights an interesting trend, with 77 percent of consumers agreeing that they would prefer to ad filter than to completely ad-block.[20] The opportunity for advertisers?

Tell—don't sell.

With more customers tuning out overtly sales-y ads, the companies that leverage advertising to be a welcome intruder on the channels they go to for news, entertainment, or community are the ones that will be the most successful.

Think of some of the most iconic ads, and you will see a common theme: they have compelling narratives—whether it's an inspirational rallying cry like Apple's Think Different or using humor to convey your message like Career Builder's Monkey Business ad, there's always a hook that pulls the viewer in. They are also personalized to the channels they live on—in this case, TV—but videos of these iconic ads have given them a second life on YouTube.

Regardless of what channel you advertise on, the key is to personalize your brand storytelling efforts with the channel's spoken rules. That, combined with the quality of your story, will provide the most relevant user experience.

Leverage sequential storytelling for your ads online. Refinery29, a lifestyle news outlet targeting women, tested a sequential storytelling campaign on Facebook with the goal of boosting its subscriber base. Over a 12-day period, Refinery29 targeted one customer segment with traditional ads and another with sequential storytelling ads that first told the brand story, then provided product information, and last invited people to subscribe. The sequential storytelling ads blew the traditional ads out of the water. Refinery29 reported an 87 percent increase in people visiting the landing page from the sequenced ads and a 56 percent increase in subscription rates.[21] In addition, the company reported the highest conversion rates among people who saw all three of the ads, as compared to just one or two, reinforcing the power of delivering brand storytelling messages in a sequence over a period of time.[22]

"Quality and engagement are critical when developing a customer base with real lifetime value," says Melissa Goidel, chief revenue officer at Refinery29. "By telling the Refinery29 story during the acquisition process, and building awareness and consideration before driving to conversion, we were able to increase our return on investment and ultimately acquire a more informed and qualified subscriber."[23]

Refinery29's sequential storytelling approach can apply to the marketing funnel, where an advertiser uses a series of messages to "walk" a potential consumer down the purchase funnel.

Alternatively, companies can pursue a priming-and-reminding storytelling approach, where an advertiser uses multiple ad formats to "prime" people with video storytelling or carousel ads. Consumers who see the awareness storytelling ads are then "reminded" of the story with follow-up ads featuring slightly different videos or images that expand on the key message to increase recall and ultimately drive sales conversions.

Blogs

We are going on record here: blogs are *not* dead! Blogs continue to make a positive impact on companies that invest in them. HubSpot analyzed blogging data from 13,500 customers and found that B2B companies that blogged 11 times or more per month had almost three times more traffic than those that blogged one time or less per month,[24] while B2C companies that blogged 11 times or more per month got more than four times as many leads as those that blogged only four to five times per month.[25]

The benefits of blogging stretch far and wide across an organization. Your blog is a dedicated channel to house customer service FAQs and your best brand stories that are easily shareable across a multitude of channels. Investing in a blog can result in increased traffic to your website, an SEO boost, press coverage, and more.

An inbound marketing and sales platform, HubSpot has benefited significantly from its corporate blog, which covers marketing, sales, agency, and customer success content. Over time, HubSpot's blog has grown to more than 400,000 subscribers and attracts over two million monthly visitors.[26]

In developing and growing its blog, HubSpot uncovered an interesting trend. The company realized that 75 percent of HubSpot's blog views and 90 percent of leads generated from its blog come from old posts.[27]

The discovery prompted HubSpot to name these top performers "compounding posts." HubSpot analyzed blogging data from more than 15,000 companies and uncovered that for most companies, 1 in 10 blog posts are compounding.[28]

To increase the likelihood of nailing a compounding post—aka the unicorn of blog posts—the key is to focus on topics designed to help readers, typically by providing instructions. HubSpot found that its top posts over-indexed on traffic and leads from customers, plus top search engine rankings.

Despite the popularity of compounding posts, HubSpot designates only about 10 percent of its blog editorial calendar to compounding posts so its content mix is more compelling. For example, one segment of customers may appreciate specific FAQs and how-to posts, while another may want to learn more about the work your company is doing in the community or the story behind a new product or service. Design your editorial calendar mix around customer insights and weight your topics and content buckets accordingly.

While the B2B space arguably over-indexes on corporate blogs, research shows that there is still significant opportunity for B2C brands. Companies like Whole Foods and Home Depot are examples of consumer brands with thriving corporate blogs. Whole Foods's blog, Whole Story, features posts about trends in the organic food space, the company's work in the community, information about its products, and delicious recipes.[29]

Home Depot's blog, on the other hand, aims to be a source of inspiration for its customers to make the most of their homes, covering DIY projects, home improvement advice, and seasonal stories.[30] What's unique about Home Depot's blog is that it invites customers to suggest topics for the company to cover, pitch themselves as contributors, or share content they have already created featuring Home Depot products for a chance to be featured on not only the blog but the company's social media channels as well.[31]

Customer Communities

Social media channels are rented land that can change or disappear at any time, so many companies are investing in dedicated customer communities. Developed by the company and hosted on a website or app owned by the brand, these communities unite customers around a common purpose, passion, or theme. They offer a dedicated place to seek information and connect with like-minded people.

Some companies use customer communities as a perk of paying for their products or services. Connect is an exclusive social community for Weight Watchers's paid members that lives on the company's app. The goal of the community is to be a safe home for members to connect with others on their weight-loss journey. From celebrating milestones, to sharing tips and providing support, Weight Watchers's customer community has become an incredibly valuable part of the company's overall product and service offering. It sees 19,000 posts a day from its members![32]

Piaggio, an Italian motor vehicle manufacturer that specializes in two-wheel motor vehicles like the iconic Vespa, sees its communities as a way to unite customers around a common passion. Piaggio's Do You Vespa? community celebrates the passion of Vespa fans who are always on the road, literally or virtually, and gives them a platform to share their stories.

You might think, "Really, a community for Vespa owners?" Oh yes! I (Jessica) experienced the passion and enthusiasm of Vespa owners firsthand when I lived in Boston. My roommate at the time owned a Vespa that she affectionately called Bessie. Not only did she love cruising the streets of Boston on her Vespa, she also regularly participated in group rides throughout the city with other Vespa owners. These group rides united Vespa owners of all ages and backgrounds around their love for the iconic vehicle. It was truly a sight to see!

The Do You Vespa? community manifesto showcases the quirky, fabulous spirit of Vespa owners:

> It may seem an odd question,
>
> But we're an odd breed aren't we?
>
> Quite happy to ride
>
> Our own path
>
> Even when it goes in the opposite direction to everyone else.
>
> Trends come and go
>
> But they're not for us.
>
> We welcome change but on our own terms.
>
> We're not trying to be different,
>
> But we know who we are
>
> And we know what we want.
>
> That's the mark of a Vespa lover.[33]

It now has over 10,000 members across 115 countries. Membership is free, but the company fosters the community through gamification by offering "Vespa points" for participating. Points can be earned by creating posters or photo strips, which is a visual way for Vespa owners to share images and stories from the rides they take on their Vespas. Other members can like and comment on these posters and photo strips. The brand also poses challenges to the community, allowing members to earn additional points. The only thing that's not really clear is what the points can be used for. Our recommendation would be for the brand to use them to identify top members to invite to VIP events and for customers to use points to redeem brand merchandise.

Often communities are created around passion points, but they do not always have to be. The key is to identify the themes or topics that are relevant to your customers. Communities can be built around a pain point, problem, life event, or serious issue.

The differentiator, though, is how you integrate experiences and meaningful connections within your community. Community management and facilitation becomes super important. If you're not sparking and encouraging regular interactions, conversations, and the sharing of ideas, the community will die. Customer communities require an investment of time and effort, but the reward is a brand-owned social network where your business is in the driver's seat and can design the experience you provide to your members.

Digital Magazines

Digital magazines are another example of "owned land." Compared to corporate blogs, online magazines tend to be more visual and topical. A key difference is also in the content shared, which is more journalistic in nature with a mix of brand and industry news, op-ed pieces, interviews, how-tos, slideshows, and more.

Several years ago, Coca-Cola redesigned its corporate website to be a digital magazine for the brand. The reason? According to Coca-Cola, the corporate website is dead. The company was inspired by the power of storytelling to cultivate engagement. Featuring content about pop culture, social media, brand history, marketing campaigns, recipes, career advice, and more, the digital magazine, called The Coca-Cola Journey, is a far cry from the traditional corporate website—in a good way.

Coca-Cola spent a year testing and understanding what types of content resonated the most with its core audience. Some of the findings were unexpected, but critical to the development of the digital magazine. In a blog post, Coca-Cola's former director of digital communications and social media, Ashley Brown, said, "The stories our readers loved surprised us month after month, and the stories we thought they would love fell flat. It was the digital equivalent of a star candidate polling below expectations."[34]

In response to consumer feedback and site data, Coca-Cola made more than 60 tweaks to the magazine, including adding sections related to food and music. The company also discovered that specific types of Coca-Cola news and information actually ranked among the top performing content! For example, background on marketing campaigns, historical stories about Coca-Cola, and information on the jobs people have within the company all generated a high level of readership, proving that company-specific stories had a relevant place in the digital magazine. As a result, the company now regularly covers company news alongside lifestyle content.

The company also mines customers' frequently asked questions to develop stories like, "What's the Difference Between Coke Zero and Coca-Cola Zero Sugar?" It also shares recipes using its products, like how to make a Coca-Cola cake. There's also the intriguing "5 Things You Never Knew About Santa Claus and Coca-Cola." All the stories, no matter how random they seem, are inspired by data and insights from fans of the brand.

The end result is a highly engaging destination with content on par with lifestyle and news websites. Every piece of content is paired with high-quality imagery, making it easy for readers to absorb what's interesting to them. As an owned asset, the magazine's content is also easy to measure, both from a page view and social sharing standpoint. During the testing phase of the redesign, Coca-Cola's Unbottled blog portion of the magazine secured a 106 percent increase in page views, while homepage visits increased by 1,247 percent, proving to the company that it was truly onto something powerful.[35]

When brands dip their toe into the publishing waters, they must keep content interesting and engaging. Full stop! The bar is higher for brands. Your editorial mission, strategy, and execution need to be well thought out if you want to be successful. Digital magazines require an ongoing investment from your company to support an editorial team, freelancers, and the resources required to produce a steady stream of engaging content. Additionally, you need to invest in ads or influencer or employee advocacy programs to amplify the content. As seen by Coca-Cola, if you want to boost customer engagement, a digital magazine can be a highly strategic way to achieve this.

Podcasts

Podcasts may be the cool new kid on the block, but did you know that they date back to the 1980s?[36] The growth of the Internet and the ubiquity of portable digital devices such as smartphones and tablets have breathed new life into podcasting. Apple Podcasts alone now has over 500,000 active podcasts, including content in more than 100 languages.[37] Edison Research found that an estimated 73 million Americans, or 26 percent of the population, listen to a podcast on a monthly basis.[38] Furthermore, the completion rate of podcasts is impressive, with 80 percent of podcast listeners completing all or most of each episode.[39]

Podcasting is an exciting medium and can take many forms, including:

Episodic Stories

General Electric, or GE, launched *The Message*, a hugely successful, eight-episode, sci-fi thriller podcast about how a top team of cryptologists attempted to decode a message received 70 years ago from outer space. GE's success with *The Message* resulted in a follow-up podcast called *LifeAfter* that draws inspiration from GE's Digital Twin technology, which creates a virtual clone of industrial machines. *LifeAfter* is a fictional 10-episode series following Ross, a low-level employee at the FBI, who chats online with his deceased wife, Charlie. Charlie passed away eight months prior, but a rogue computer program is bringing loved ones back to life through virtual cloning, taking people like Ross down a dangerous path.

Educational Content

With the goal of making cyber-security issues easier to understand, entertaining, and educational, McAfee created Hackable, an appropriately titled podcast that pulls famous hacks from news headlines, as well as popular TV shows and movies, and puts them to the test in real-life experiments. Episodes are 25 minutes long and cover how to hack a webcam, the Wi-Fi at a cafe, or the computer of a moving vehicle. They feature cyber security experts and hackers, adding credibility to the podcast.

In its first season, Hackable attracted over 72,000 subscribers and generated over 920,000 downloads across 10 episodes.[40] It was the number one tech news podcast and the third ranked technology podcast on Apple Podcast's U.S. charts.[41] The show become so popular, it was picked up by SiriusXM Insights. McAfee decided to renew it for a second season. As a result of the podcast, research revealed that 79 percent of listeners are able to identify McAfee as the sponsor of the podcast,[42] while 65 percent said they now have a higher opinion of the McAfee brand, showcasing the power of podcasting to increase brand credibility on topics that are core to your business.

Topical Advice

Podcasts also offer a strong opportunity for offering advice on or insights into a topic of interest that's aligned with your business. Now in its second season, eBay's podcast *Open for Business* provides tips on and stories about building a business from the ground up. With so much advice already out there, eBay's goal was to focus the podcast on the little-known stories that offer valuable lessons about starting or running a small business. With episodes on the gig economy, hiring, bootstrapping your business, and more, the first season of *Open for Business* was ranked number one among business podcasts on iTunes.[43]

Product Announcements

While the majority of companies invest in entire and multiple podcast seasons, a few have done short-term podcasts. McDonald's partnered with The Onion and Gizmodo to launch a three-episode podcast called *The Sauce*, which tells the story of what went wrong with the company's limited rerelease of its Szechuan McNugget dipping sauce in October 2017. The Szechuan McNugget dipping sauce became famous with the company's millennial customers after it was featured in the season three premiere of the popular show *Rick and Morty*.

It quickly became apparent to McDonald's that a super limited rerelease of the Szechuan McNugget dipping sauce was not going to cut it after passionate fans camped out overnight and traveled long distances in search of the coveted sauce. To make amends and promote that 20 million packets of Szechuan sauce would be available across all US McDonald's restaurants as of February 26, 2018, the company launched *The Sauce* podcast to tell the story of its mistakes and answer questions, offering valuable transparency to its customers. The decision to tell this story through a podcast was incredibly popular, with *The Sauce* peaking at number 94 on the iTunes 100 podcast list less than 24 hours after its release, which is no small feat.[44]

With more companies pursuing podcasting as part of their brand storytelling content mix, here are four key tips to evaluate as you consider this exciting medium:

1. **Nobody Wants to Listen to a Brand Commercial**
   Podcasting is inherently a more personal medium.
   Listeners decide when to tune in, and if they do,
   they are investing one-on-one time with your
   brand. The level of immersion and frequency
   makes podcasting a tempting medium for companies. However, as the previous examples illustrate,
   the quality bar is incredibly high for branded
   podcasts. Nobody wants to listen to a brand commercial. Companies must think about how they
   can differentiate themselves through compelling stories, thought-provoking topics, or valuable
   advice that set them apart from other podcasts.

2. **Be Consumable on the Go**
   Research shows that 69 percent of podcast listeners tune in via portable devices like smartphones
   and tablets.[45] They tend to consume all or most of
   the podcast, but they tend to do so when they need
   to be hands-free. Whether the listener is getting
   things done at home, working out, or commuting,
   make sure to design the content, format, and flow
   of your podcasts to be easily consumable while
   hands-free or on the go.

3. **Partner with the Pros**
   All the podcasts cited share something in common: they were all cocreated with companies that
   specialize in making podcasts with brands. While
   companies could, in theory, create their own podcasts in-house, a successful podcast requires more
   than a good mic and a conference room to record
   it in. It also demands a significant time commitment. Most podcasts have a daily or weekly release

schedule, meaning that once you start, you need
to deliver or risk losing your audience. Before you
dive headfirst into the podcasting waters, make
sure you understand what it truly takes to deliver
a best-in-class product.

4. **Invest in the Long Game**
   A podcast is an investment in the long game. NPR
   found that while 75 percent of podcast listeners take
   an action on a sponsored message, a consumer still
   needs to hear that message 25 to 30 times before a
   conversion happens.[46] That means when companies invest in their own podcasts, the goal should be
   to build brand awareness and connections, not an
   immediate sale or new business lead. Additionally,
   simply creating a podcast and putting it online isn't
   enough. As podcasting increases in popularity, companies need to invest in the ongoing marketing and
   advertising of their podcasts to ensure that their target audience actually knows of their existence.

5. **Consistency Is Key**
   Brands have a bad habit of starting something
   and not seeing it through. If you decide to start a
   podcast, stay with it. Decide on a release schedule
   and don't waver. People expect you to post with
   the promised frequency, so if you post weekly on
   Fridays, stick with it. That is what your listeners
   expect, and that's what will help you build your
   audience over time.

Voice Assistants

The rise of podcasting is just one piece of the puzzle
when it comes to the booming popularity of voice.

According to the Consumer Technology Association, sales of smart speakers like Amazon Echo and Google Home jumped 237 percent in 2017.[47] Juniper Research predicts that by 2022, 55 percent of US households will have smart speaker devices, but expansion across other platforms like cars, connected TVs, and wearable devices will increase the use of voice assistant devices by 95 percent.[48] At present, Adobe's research shows that 54 percent of consumers with a voice assistant use them daily, with the top use cases being music, weather, directions, information queries, setting alarms or reminders, and shopping.[49]

With more consumers incorporating voice assistants into their lives, companies have taken notice, building skills that offer a voice concierge type of service. BMW, for example, created the BMW Connected skill to support drivers of its 2014 model vehicles through the present in the United States. The skill is a companion to its BMW Connected mobile app, with the goal of improving the overall BMW driving experience. While in the car, the BMW Connected skill allows drivers or passengers to use their voice to lock the doors, manipulate the climate control, make sure the windows are up, check how much gas is left, and more.[50]

The Tide Stain Remover skill has quickly become a top Alexa skill by helping people get out of sticky or messy situations, literally. Consumers use the Tide Stain Remover skill for step-by-step voice instructions on how to remove over 200 types of stains. The skill has gained praise for also offering to send the directions to the Alexa app or in a text to the user's mobile phone.[51]

With voice assistants still in their infancy stage, the best practice for businesses is to align skills with a customer benefit by providing valuable information customers could need while on the go or a time-saver for a highly repetitive task, like reordering a specific item. That's not to say that businesses cannot be creative with their skills, using them to shape stories or positive customer experiences.

Johnnie Walker's skill offers a strong blend of educational and experiential content. Consumers can learn about the brand's whiskey varieties, perhaps to help them purchase the perfect one for themselves or as a gift. Its Alexa skill can also take customers step-by-step through a guided Johnnie Walker tasting, offering a more robust brand storytelling element.[52]

Warner Bros. has taken a completely different approach to its Alexa skill with The Wayne Investigation video game. Described as a mystery game, listeners can play detective and investigate the murder of Thomas and Martha Wayne, Batman's parents. The game boasts an average rating of 4.5, and users rave about the clever voices, writing, and immersiveness the skill provides family members of different ages. Users report spending at least 30 minutes navigating the various paths and right/wrong choices needed to correctly solve the murder mystery.[53]

For companies looking to develop their own skills, consider the following best practices:

1. **Shape Skills around Customer Needs**
   Look closely at the top skills, and you will see a theme: they provide value quickly and efficiently in the moment. From reordering products, to locking doors or solving problems, making customers' lives easier has been a must when developing a brand skill.

2. **It's All about the Listening Experience**
   The right audio elements and mix are a key differentiator when it comes to how customers perceive
   your skill. Don't scrimp here. Spend time testing
   and understanding all the elements, from the voice
   talent to the sound effects, that will influence the
   customer experience.

3. **Stay True to Your Voice—and Keep It Consistent**
   Your voice goes far beyond just sound. The voice
   you use on voice assistants or skills needs to be consistent with how you speak to or communicate with
   customers across other channels. Be true to yourself—and let your unique brand personality shine
   through. The more you can integrate the experience
   you provide to customers across your other touchpoints, the more discoverable and useful it will be.

4. **Don't Overbrand or Overadvertise**
   While the Tide Stain Remover skill gets positive
   ratings for its advice, many users negatively call
   out the ads as too long and annoying. With skills,
   brands should prioritize adding value over advertising. The more you can help, the more likely you
   are to achieve your goals, so ditch ads that do not
   add value to the customer experience.

5. **Establish Your Base, but Don't Be Afraid to Be Creative**
   Start with skills that add value, but take inspiration
   from Warner Bros. and Johnnie Walker. As your
   brand grows a strong presence, explore experiential
   skills. From step-by-step immersive experiences
   to choose-your-own-adventure stories, allow your
   creative juices to flow.

Chapter 6

THE LAWS OF ENGAGEMENT

ENGAGE WITH YOUR COMMUNITIES

Engagement is the heart of marketing.

This is arguably the most important chapter in the book. Why? Because the best strategy and the most compelling content will fade into nothingness without meaningful social interaction. Social interaction is what starts the conversation, amplifies the discussion by bringing more people into the fold of your brand, and, if you are lucky, sparks something bigger.

If communities are the pulse of your brand, then engagement is your lifeblood.

Communities mean different things to different people. So let's define the word *community*. A community is a group of people united by the same goals, interests, and attitudes. Social networks, digital forums, and closed brand communities offer platforms for groups of people to get together virtually and discuss shared topics of interest. Communities are composed of a variety of different groups: customers, employees, shareholders, partners, and so on.

A brand is either the host or a guest of those communities. Usually it's the latter. Communities hosted by brands are considered more of a marketing ploy than an authentic place for transparent conversations—but there are exceptions to the rules.

Engagement powers communities. Without consistent and relevant engagement, a community would be short-lived. Communities, in turn, power the conversations around the themes that matter to brands, as well as serving as catalysts for sparking real movements.

Let's look at the laws of engagement.

THE RESPONSE LAW

As a brand, if you are not listening on digital platforms, that is a problem. If you are not engaging with consumers when they initiate conversations with you, you don't exist. Your competitors do, however.

If you *are* listening and you *are* engaging, good for you. Now, do it better!

When we meet with executives, it's crazy when we still have to convince them that they have no choice but to be present digitally. However, that is still the case. According to Sprout Social consumer survey, 90 percent of people have used social media platforms to communicate directly with a brand. Not surprising, since social surpasses phone and e-mail as the first place most people turn when they have an issue with a product or service. In spite of the high volume of messages that require a response, brands reply to just 11 percent of people (this number hasn't changed since 2015). The result? Thirty-six percent will shame you publicly, while one in three will switch to a competitor.[1]

So when executives ask us: "What is the risk of engaging?" our answer is "The better question would be: what's the risk of *not* engaging?"

So you are present. Now what?

Follow the 80/20 rule. Remember that social engagement does not equal promotion (hint: look up the definition of the word *social*). You've provided a platform for your communities to engage with you. That comes with great responsibility. It isn't another advertising channel. It isn't about you, it is about *them*. So design your engagement strategy so that 80 percent of the content you share is of value to your audience and only 20 percent of the content is promotional in nature (reserved for when you launch a new product line or have a big announcement).

And respond to everyone. Yes, everyone! There is only one exception: trolls.

In building your response strategy, consider:

- Brand inquiries
- Product inquiries
- Customer care inquiries
- Crisis inquiries
- Executive inquiries

Your engagement strategy should include creating content pieces or crafting engagement questions that are relevant and interesting to your communities. Refer to Chapter 4, "The Story-Making Laws," for more information and ideas on this topic.

Now, let's focus on something a lot of brands and community managers fear: angry customers.

Nobody wants negative reviews or comments floating around on social channels. According to Econsultancy, one to three negative reviews is all it takes to deter the majority of shoppers from purchasing a product or service.[2] But all of that changes if a brand makes an effort to apologize and fix the issue:

- 68 percent of users say the presence of a management response to negative reviews sways them toward purchasing from that company[3]
- 34 percent of customers delete their negative review or write a revision after the company reaches out to them with an apology[4]

It's incredible to think that a simple response or apology can prevent customers from switching brands.

In our humble opinion, every negative comment is a golden opportunity to turn a detractor into an advocate.

To effectively address and resolve complaints on social, simply remember these **three As:**

Acknowledge

A complaint warrants a prompt response. Nearly 40 percent of people expect a response within an hour on social media, while the average brand response rate is closer to five hours.[5]

If your brand can bridge the gap between consumer expectations and reality, you've already taken the first step to improving your customers' experience. Immediately acknowledging a person, even if you are still working on the solution, goes a long way.

Apologize

Don't just apologize. Mean it!

Authenticity is the key ingredient to an apology, both online and offline. Be genuine. Avoid a cookie-cutter apology. Remember, you are talking to someone who is having a tough day because your product or service didn't deliver. At a minimum, give your customers the respect and empathy they deserve.

Personalize your interaction when you can, and make sure they know that they matter to you.

The only caveat here is when there is current or potential legal action against your brand. In such cases, make sure to consult your company's legal counsel to approve any responses and ensure that they are aligned with how the company is handling the issue or lawsuit.

Act

Acting on a complaint is the most critical step, as failing to do so would negate the apology.

Resolve the issue. Don't just say you'll fix it, actually do it. If you don't know how to fix it, find someone within your company who does (that's what the process/team flowcharts are for). Be prepared.

Once you do resolve the problem, ask yourself if this warrants an internal blog post so that anyone else who is experiencing the same difficulty can take advantage of the information. This will save the company a lot of time and resources.

Beyond a specific response or fix, look at this process in the context of your brand's broader social media management and ask:

- Do you have a response service level agreement (SLA)/goal in place?

- Are the right people responding to complaints?
- Are they utilizing the right technology (queues, routing, escalation, governance, etc.) that helps streamline the process?
- Is there appropriate messaging in place (templates, content libraries)?

If you ace the three As, imagine the stories your customers will be telling about you. Storytelling isn't just about carefully crafted brand messages created by your marketing team. The most impactful brand storytelling comes from satisfied customers eager to tell their friends about your amazing service and product.

Airlines exemplify real-time issue resolution on social networks. We don't remember the last time we had to call an airline to get an answer when something went wrong in our travels. While people line up in front of a customer service agent at the airport, it only takes us several minutes to get a status update from an airline or get rebooked on the next available flight. Social media is becoming the most efficient mechanism to get ahold of an agent. Royal Dutch Airlines KLM, for example, tells you right in its Twitter bio that its social care team is available in 10 languages. And its account is marked "responsive 24/7," which is not dissimilar to the rest of the major airlines you look up on Twitter. KLM's targeted response time ranges from 5 to 15 minutes. And now a number of airlines use messenger apps and chatbots to offer that service in even less time.

If you are wondering what the return on investment is for airlines besides top-notch customer care (shouldn't that be enough?), consider that KLM is making €25 million per year from social media! Not only that, by listening to and engaging with its customers it innovates in the coolest ways. Example? By monitoring the feedback on social media, the company unearthed the demand for social payments, which it then implemented. Its new social payments tool cost €3,500 to set up and now accounts for €80,000 per week in sales.[6]

When it comes to stimulating conversations, there is no one better than Wendy's. Whether it is rapping, sassing people who name-drop fast-food competitors, or troll roasting, Wendy's attention-grabbing tweets are highly entertaining. And when customers reach out with a complaint, Wendy's social media team doesn't just produce the average "I am sorry to hear that" response, but creates personalized witty tweets that make you smile. Wendy's sass strategy is addictive, and people engage with the brand often just to hear the team's snappy comebacks.

Here are just some of the priceless exchanges:

@niickba: @Wendys Spit some bars

@Wendys: Barbecue and ranch, ranch and sweet and sour, dipping chicken nuggets, hour after hour.

@ltshex1c: @Wendys My friend wants to go to McDonald's. What should I tell him?

@Wendys: Find new friends

@KrypticH4wk: If I don't have a @Wendys at my location, what do I do?!?

@Wendys: Move

@SalernoBailey: Why is your beef square?

@Wendys: Because we don't cut corners

@AliAlTuhafi: @Wendys how many monkeys do you have that make up your social media team?

@Wendys: The monkeys are busy writing Shakespeare. We are a team of advanced pop culture robots

@Carladelreyy: @Wendys What should I get from McDonald's????

@Wendys: Directions to the nearest Wendy's

@LacedILouie: @Wendys Roast me

@Wendys: Get one of your 51 followers to roast you

@LacedILouie: I am going to @BurgerKing now

@Wendys: Now you are just punishing yourself

@Ysys0204: Going to In n Out. What should I get?

@Wendys: Out

THE SURPRISE AND DELIGHT LAW

Being present and engaged is the first step.

To show your customers you care, go above and beyond. Just like REI did when it sent me (Ekaterina) the custom video response to my gift question on Twitter.

Just like Citi Bike did when Paull Young fell off the bike. Literally.

At the time, Paull was the director of digital at charity: water. One morning he hopped on a Citi Bike and headed to work. It was raining lightly that day, and as he was rounding a corner, the bike slid from under him and he fell. So he tweeted: "Started my day falling off my @citibikeNYC in the rain #HappyFriday." His friend Ryan asked him if he was OK, to which he jokingly replied: "@RyanZorro17 @CitibikeNYC bro my khakis are all messed up #PLEASESENDPANTS." A few hours later when he got out of his meetings, a colleague handed him a package from Citi Bike. In it were several J. Crew gift cards! Then he spotted this tweet from @CitiBikeNYC: "@paullyoung Stay tuned, help is on the way via @jcrew! #PANTSFORPAULL." It made his day. In his blog post about his #PANTSFORPAULL experience, Paull says: "I love this so much. I'm already a huge fan of Citi Bike, and now I'm a new J. Crew customer. Marketing is all about relationships, and every relationship needs to have mutual benefit."[7]

We all hear those amazing stories of extraordinary customer service. Zappos, for example, is continuously cited as the leader in this department. Whether you are looking for shoes or the closest pizza joint, you will get help finding it if you call Zappos. However, the unfortunate truth is that most of us do not experience extraordinary customer service very often. What's more disappointing is that some of us have never experienced it at all.

For my (Ekaterina's) mother-in-law, Lauri, it took 68 years to encounter amazing customer service. A while back, I bought her a bra from Soma Intimates. It was exactly what she was looking for. A year or so later, she tried to replace it without success as it had been discontinued. Unbeknownst to me, she wrote a letter to Soma to express her disappointment. It was a handwritten letter. My mother-in-law doesn't use social media.

Imagine her surprise when two weeks later, she received a call from the company's representative, informing her that the company had received her letter and leaders had discussed it at their weekly corporate meeting. The result? They were going to look in every store across the country for the bra she wanted. A week later, she received a package containing seven—the last seven left in the country! With it came a handwritten letter from a store manager, an appropriate way to communicate with this customer, through the channel she had used.

It said:

Dear Lauri,

Our corporate office called saying you had been searching for a Sofia bra. I was happy to find these at my outlet for you! They have been discontinued and perhaps are the last ones in our company. I hope you enjoy these. They are being sent to you complimentary from our corporate office.

Our love and best wishes,
Sue Peters
Store Mgr #5287, Jersey Shore Premium Outlets

"I started being rather disappointed with the company," Lauri told me afterward. "Now, I would never say anything negative about it. Actually, I will be recommending it to all my female friends. What a delightful experience!"

What is most remarkable about this story is the company's attention to a woman who isn't an influencer with thousands of followers, and the fact that it didn't matter to this company. That is the true definition of an amazing brand.

Lauri's satisfaction was priority number one for Soma. Me sharing her experience with hundreds of thousands of people through a post on Fast Company and subsequently in a number of my keynote speeches is just icing on the cake for Soma, as are all of the additional customers our family has referred to the brand over the years.

Mind you, that year I switched from Victoria's Secret to Soma Intimates, and I haven't gone back since.

I know we talk a lot about online storytelling. But once again, we must remind you that storytelling goes beyond online conversations and touches every part of your business, from packaging and distribution to customer care and beyond. In their 2012 title *The Face-to-Face Book: Why Real Relationships Rule in a Digital Marketplace*, Ed Keller and Bray Fay state that 90 percent of all conversations about brands happen offline. In the United States that number hasn't changed much year over year. Face-to-face interactions are still the preferred method of communication for human beings and some of the best—and worst—brand stories are shared offline.

We know what you are thinking right now: "Is the surprise and delight approach scalable?" No! It isn't. Not in the way you think. You cannot give every customer a free pair of pants, but what you can do is give each customer your attention and respect. You can train every single one of your employees (yes, every single one) to engage your customers on a human level. At Mercedes, every single employee understands that customer delight is their number one priority, even if they don't interact directly with the customer in their daily jobs. If they can do anything at all to improve the process, the product, or the service in a way that makes the customer happy, they do it. After all, what happens behind the scenes matters just as much as on the front line. Maybe even more so.

Moreover, it is a well-known fact that people relate to other people's experiences as though they were their own. So when Paull's community sees that Citi Bike helped him out of a bind, they appreciate it just as much as they would have had it happened to them. They celebrate it. And they remember it. And that story will live on, told and retold. Why? Because for some of us, exceptional customer service only happens once in a blue moon.

Now you are probably asking: "How do we do it? Do we wait until something bad happens to try the surprise-and-delight tactic? Do we comb the Internet looking for opportunities that might lead to a great story?" You can. A good digital listening tool will help with not only getting ahead of a potential crisis, but finding potential opportunities to surprise and delight. But how about being proactive about it? Follow the examples of Grand Hyatt and Residence Inn and proactively ask your customers what they want—and then deliver it!

Here is a story told to us by our friend and fellow digital marketer Eric Tung:

> Ever wonder if companies read those extra request boxes on their forms?
>
> Well, Manchester Grand Hyatt San Diego does.
>
> When I arrived in San Diego for the conference, I found this in my hotel room: a box of crayons, a picture of a pickle, and a Snickers bar. [See Figure 6.1.]

FIGURE 6.1 Manchester Grand Hyatt San Diego surprises and delights a guest

The accompanying note read:

"Dear Eric Tung,

Welcome! When we were looking over your reservation we noticed that you were requesting a picture of a pickle and a piece of chocolate to enjoy. Here at the Manchester Grand Hyatt San Diego we want to make sure your needs aren't just met, they are exceeded. Have fun coloring in this pickle and enjoy your time at the Social Media Marketing World Conference 2015! Let us know if you need anything else.

Sincerely,
Manchester Grand Hyatt San Diego"

I was pleasantly surprised. By both the attention to detail and by the extra effort the staff put into making my stay not only pleasant, but fun.

So I shared my delight on social networks and my community loved being a part (if even distant) of such an amazing experience.

But the story wasn't over.

Another company was listening as well.

Six days later I walked into my Residence Inn hotel room in Florida and found this nice little surprise: [See Figure 6.2.]

FIGURE 6.2   Residence Inn in Florida raises the stakes

The accompanying note read:

"Mr. Tung,

Heard you like pickles and chocolate. Am I doing this right? Thanks for staying with us and have fun on Amelia!

Amy,
Residence Inn Staff"

I was floored that another hotel chain all the way in Florida was even aware of my experience in San Diego. But what was even cooler was that when I tweeted saying the Residence Inn Amelia might have "one-upped" Grand Hyatt, they replied with: "No one-upping here—we were inspired by them! Always <3 seeing great hospitality provided. #differentlogosameteam." THAT was truly fantastic to see!

Today, too many companies take customers for granted. It's almost refreshing when you get basic customer service, and surprising when you get exceptional service.

Little things matter. They show that companies pay attention to their customers. Because if they get the little things right, there's a good chance that the big things will be right as well.

It was said that the rock band Van Halen used to write into their tour contracts that they wanted a bowl of M&M's with the brown ones removed in their dressing room at every venue. It wasn't because they were picky; it was to ensure that the venue managers read the full contract carefully.

In an age when an offhand tweet or poorly timed campaign can mean doom for a brand, companies need to show their human side more than ever.

■ THE LAW OF HUMANIZING YOUR BRAND ■

If you made a mistake, for the love of all that's holy, please stop backpedaling and trying to get out of it. Just apologize.

People want to do business with people, not faceless corporations. Don't be afraid to admit your failings and show empathy whenever possible. Doing so will remind your customers that there are actual people behind your logo. And you will see your brand story taking on a different meaning. From a negative and soulless experience to a human connection, the story and perception of your company will morph into one of respect and trust. When a company does right by us consistently, it becomes part of our trusted network.

We have discussed this at length in the Response Law, so we won't revisit it in too much detail. However, this law extends beyond just admitting fault or helping customers in their moments of distress. Here are other ways to humanize your brand:

Identify Your Reps by Name

Consider having your community managers identify themselves in their social media communications. Some sign each tweet with their full names. Some just put their initials at the end (example: ^jg or ^cd). I (Ekaterina) am a huge fan of Alaska Airlines. It's my number one choice for travel and has been for almost 20 years. How big of a fan? Let's just say that I don't get starstruck easily, but when I met the CEO of Alaska Airlines, Brad Tilden, I just had to take a picture (Figure 6.3). I swear I know most of their social care agents by name. Most of my interactions are with Angel. Always on top of it, Angel has been answering critical questions and helping me solve minor issues for years. To me, Angel is the face of the company. Alaska Air social care agents always sign their first names. Tweet at them and see for yourself.

FIGURE 6.3   Ekaterina with Brad Tilden,
CEO of Alaska Airlines

Be Transparent on Big Issues

It's easy to default to a corporate response or take your most sensitive brand questions and issues offline. However, if a negative issue or perception comes up time and time again, why not tackle it head-on? Plagued by constant questions and misconceptions about the ingredients in its food, McDonald's launched the "Our Food. Your Questions." campaign in Canada, where the brand answered more than 20,000 questions in six months. Over that period, McDonald's Canada generated 10 million interactions online, with engagement of over four minutes per visit. Furthermore, monthly store visits grew by 50 percent, prompting the company to take the campaign stateside.[8] The initiative is a great reminder that answering customer inquiries can translate into transformative brand marketing and storytelling initiatives that humanize your brand.

Don't Just Solve Problems, Provide Value and Help

Birchbox is a great example. When Snapchat first announced new video calling features within the app, the Birchbox social media customer service team decided to run a test. For one hour, fans could call them through Snapchat and ask questions. The calls resulted in a light bulb moment for the brand. The Birchbox team realized that many of the callers were looking for more personalized makeup and skincare advice. The experiment prompted the company to host live, face-to-face calls with customers on a regular cadence. This concept is not new. Hotels offer concierge services so travelers have a better experience at their properties and in the cities they're visiting. Why not include a more personalized concierge service in your brand strategy? It doesn't just apply to B2C brands. B2B brands have a huge, untapped opportunity to help customers and prospects be better at their jobs through consultative problem-solving and advisory services.

Ultimately, if you prioritize giving over selling, your company will win every time.

Invite Customers In by Showcasing Your Culture

While responsiveness and empathy are imperative, another important element in humanizing your brand comes from showcasing your culture. Consider taking a page from Cisco's playbook here. The company shares its company culture through the #WeAreCisco campaign where employee brand evangelists partner with the company's Talent Brand Social Team to take over specific social media channels like Snapchat, Twitter, and Instagram. Although Cisco's goal is to make personal connections with future talent, the spirit of this campaign extends far beyond human resources and appeals to current clients, prospects, and corporate partners. With Cisco's overarching company mission to "shape the future of the Internet," the #WeAreCisco campaign puts a human face on how the company is doing this through the micro moments and personal stories from its talented and inspiring employees.

Chapter 7

OH, ONE MORE LAW . . .

MAKE YOUR OWN

Are you ready? This one is a doozy.

The last law is . . . *There are no absolute laws!*

If you want to innovate, you have to step outside of the tried-and-trues, the they-did-it-and-it-worked traps, and the it-is-safer-that-way excuses. When it comes to doing something remarkable, there are no laws, rules, or case studies. If others have already done it, *they* are the leaders, not you. You have to defy the norm, throw out the rules, and come up with your own. Yes, you have to be reasonable, even cautious in some cases. Yes, you have to consider the basics, the lessons we have shared with you. But you also have to trust your gut and try the crazy, the weird, the different.

"Know the rules well, so you can break them effectively." —Dalai Lama XIV

Where to start?
Here are some of our suggestions:

1. **Don't Benchmark against Your Competition or Your Industry Peers**
   They are not your true competitors. Other innovators and disruptors are. Those disruptors are the ones who define and redefine what great branding, marketing, and storytelling are and should be.

2. **Focus on Your Most Passionate Fans**
   When crafting your stories, don't try to appeal to everyone. Make your stories relevant to your niche, your most passionate followers, your best customer segment, no matter how small. Connect with them, spark conversations, hear what they have to say, bring them into the fold. Build from there.

3. **Seek Inspiration Elsewhere**
   Look to other industries, brands, geographies, and small businesses that are truly remarkable at telling stories and engaging with their communities. Find who does it well (it isn't that hard), figure out how they do it, and model the behavior. Don't copy, but apply the blueprint to your company/industry/situation/product.

4. Become Obsessed

Never stop learning. Expand your network, talk to other storytellers, seek the know-how from those who already walked your path, read. Great storytelling is an art. It doesn't just happen. You have to love what you do. You have to love your brand. You have to know your product. You have to respect your customers. You have to understand your tribe. The coolest thing about art is that it is fluid; it is never set in stone. It has many angles, many perspectives, many approaches. Find yours.

5. Be a Rebel

Do the things that are "just not done." Defy the average and the norm. Live the mantra "Safe is risky." Ask, "What if?" and "Why not?" every day.

6. Execute

Ideas are worthless unless executed. Choose the one you think is worth experimenting with and implement it. Start small; do a pilot in one geography or with one department. Test it, learn, perfect it. Then share the results, market the idea internally, and roll it out globally. Find stakeholders who are willing to champion, support, and fund your idea. And remember that sometimes you succeed by not asking for permission. Ask for forgiveness later.

Above all, never ever settle for easy, expected, and conventional.

CONCLUSION

The rules of brand storytelling are changing. With the evolution of social networks, the unspoken etiquette of digital communities, and consumer expectations comes a seismic shift in how we source, create, and share our stories.

In this book we discussed the biggest changes we have seen to date and what you can do to address them. We won't recap them here. Instead, we want to remind you—regardless of your role, the industry you are in, or the size of your company—of the mentality shifts that are necessary to become a great brand storyteller:

From Brand-Centric to Customer-Centric

It's not about you; it's about them. Create stories that your audience can relate to. Make your customer the hero. Be human in everything you do.

From Marketing to Customer Experience

Brand storytelling isn't a marketing function. It is an impression you create at every single touchpoint of the customer experience journey. From product packaging to customer care, everything you do—and how you do it—becomes a story. It becomes your brand. It's not just about the stories you tell; it's also about the stories your customers create after they engage with you.

From Head Marketing to Heart Marketing

We have no doubt your product is great, but your product isn't what will make consumers buy from you. They want to know who you are and what you stand for. Modern consumers are more conscious of the company's bigger impact on the people and environment around them. Telling your prospective buyers all about the features and functions of your products isn't enough anymore. You have to open your kimono and show them the humanity behind the brand. You have to share your mission, your passions, and your struggles. Data and proof points appeal to our brains, but authentic stories appeal to our hearts. Be the kind of storyteller who tells the latter.

From Story to Action

Don't just talk the talk. Walk the walk. Don't just produce content to pacify consumers. Back it up with action. Brand storytelling isn't just about the content you create. Brand storytelling is about who you are. It's about aligning your actions with your purpose and delivering on the promises you make to your customers.

The rules of brand storytelling are changing. Yet one simple, but powerful truth stays the same:

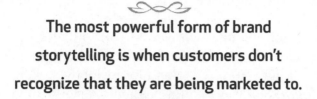

The most powerful form of brand storytelling is when customers don't recognize that they are being marketed to.

In this book we presented 30 rules of brand storytelling.

Now go and make your own!

The Beginning

ACKNOWLEDGMENTS

First and foremost, we would like to thank you, the reader, for picking up our book. We hope you found everything you were looking for inside.

We have always had a passion for storytelling. We believe that something truly magical happens when you hear a story that strikes a chord in you. We want to extend our sincerest gratitude to the many inspiring storytellers we've encountered throughout our lives, from family, to friends, colleagues, brand storytellers, novelists, and more. You are a gift in more ways than you can ever know. Thank you for sparking our imagination.

We would like to offer our deepest gratitude to the extraordinary people who shared this journey with us. Rebecca Takada, for being a go-to creative resource for us and for her beautiful opening chapter designs. Chris Buehler and the creative team at his agency Scorch, for their invaluable creative direction on our cover. The fantastic team at McGraw-Hill, who have shared our giddy excitement over this book from the beginning and have been with us every step of the way.

Most important, we are thankful for our families, who encouraged and supported us along this journey. We do not say this enough: you are our rock! Our accomplishments are your accomplishments.

As you turn the final pages of this book, hopefully energized and inspired to craft your own stories, we would like to invite you to share your thoughts and your storytelling adventures with us. Drop us a note at guidetobrandstorytelling@gmail.com. We are always happy to make new friends.

NOTES

Introduction

1. https://hbr.org/2012/12/your-companys-history-as-a-leadership-tool.
2. https://www.youtube.com/watch?v=IMsxrJeJ8lU.

Chapter 1

1. https://www.youtube.com/watch?v=lqewBwv4xyw.
2. https://www.youtube.com/watch?v=ZUG9qYTJMsl.
3. http://www.jessicagioglio.com/why-zappos-wants-to-make-leap-day-a-national-holiday/.
4. https://open.buffer.com/buffer-values/.
5. https://business.tutsplus.com/tutorials/how-to-define-your-core-brand-values-and-why-you-should--cms-26301.
6. https://www.virgin.com/entrepreneur/how-richard-bransons-dyslexia-shaped-virgins-values.
7. https://www.slideshare.net/HubSpot/the-hubspot-culture-code-creating-a-company-we-love?ref=https://www.hubspot.com/careers-blog/how-we-fixed-a-critical-bug-in-hubspots-culture-code.
8. https://www.hubspot.com/careers-blog/how-we-fixed-a-critical-bug-in-hubspots-culture-code.
9. http://adage.com/article/behind-the-work/gap-wrong/146393/.
10. https://www.theguardian.com/media/2010/oct/12/gap-logo-redesign.
11. http://www.canny-creative.com/10-rebranding-failures-how-much-they-cost/.
12. https://www.colormatters.com/component/content/article?id=240:color-a-branding.
13. https://thelogocompany.net/blog/infographics/psychology-color-logo-design/.
14. http://www.dailymail.co.uk/video/news/video-1172270/The-original-epic-strut-Money-Supermarket.html.
15. https://www.youtube.com/watch?v=G3GhWh68AL4.
16. https://www.goodreads.com/quotes/792897-your-smile-is-your-logo-your-personality-is-your-business.

17. http://www.convinceandconvert.com/social-media-case
    -studies/cant-miss-campaign-your-year-with-nike/.
18. https://www.socialmediatoday.com/news/survey-finds
    -consumers-crave-authenticity-and-user-generated-content
    -deli/511360/.
19. http://www.adweek.com/brand-marketing/here-are-the
    -4-biggest-brand-marketing-trends-at-advertising-week/.
20. http://www.dailymail.co.uk/femail/article-3689385/Tesco
    -customer-complains-hollow-scotch-egg-receives-poetic
    -reply.html.
21. http://www.dailymail.co.uk/femail/article-3689385/Tesco
    -customer-complains-hollow-scotch-egg-receives-poetic
    -reply.html.
22. https://www.youtube.com/watch?v=2xeanX6xnRU.
23. https://www.fastcompany.com/3048348/how-honey-maid
    -brought-wholesome-family-values-into-the-21st-century.
24. https://www.fastcompany.com/3048348/how-honey-maid
    -brought-wholesome-family-values-into-the-21st-century.
25. https://www.thunderclap.it/projects/9666-this-is
    -wholesome.
26. https://consumerist.com/2014/04/03/honey-maid-is-okay
    -with-people-hating-its-ad-showing-wholesome-gay
    -parents/.
27. https://www.newyorker.com/business/currency/honey-maid
    -and-the-business-of-love.
28. https://sproutsocial.com/insights/data/championing-change
    -in-the-age-of-social-media/.
29. https://www.youtube.com/watch?v=yetFk7QoSck.
30. https://www.airbnb.co.uk/weaccept.
31. https://marketing.atairbnb.com/casestudies/we-accept.
32. https://press.atairbnb.com/about-us/.
33. https://sproutsocial.com/insights/data/championing-change
    -in-the-age-of-social-media/.
34. https://www.ge.com/reports/engineering-future-ges-goal
    -bridge-stem-gender-gap-2020/.
35. https://www.ge.com/reports/engineering-future-ges-goal
    -bridge-stem-gender-gap-2020/.
36. http://www.adweek.com/brand-marketing/ge-imagines
    -a-world-where-we-treat-female-scientists-like-celebrities/.
37. https://www.nytimes.com/2017/02/23/science/mildred
    -dresselhaus-dead-queen-of-carbon.html.

38. https://twitter.com/DoomBucky/status/661038366125895680.
39. https://twitter.com/shelflife_shop/status/665707890917941249.
40. https://twitter.com/sarbear0130/status/669690049865375745.
41. https://twitter.com/reeses/status/672120819586342912.
42. https://twitter.com/reeses/status/672492207727857664.
43. https://twitter.com/reeses/status/675743190922747904.
44. https://twitter.com/reeses/status/676869242860544000.
45. https://twitter.com/stephjillcartin/status/676544435551735809.
46. https://vimeo.com/177441941.

Chapter 2

1. http://annexneversleeps.com/about/.
2. https://www.nkdwine.com/nkd-story/.

Chapter 3

1. http://startupquotes.startupvitamins.com/post/77385350314/your-brand-is-what-other-people-say-about-you.
2. https://www.wired.com/2009/08/radioshack-rebrands-as-the-shack/.
3. https://www.engadget.com/2009/08/02/radio-shack-rebranding-to-the-shack/.
4. http://www.technologizer.com/2009/08/03/nin-reasons-radioshack-shouldnt-change-its-name/.
5. http://adage.com/article/news/radioshack-shack-a-marketing-nickname/138297/.
6. https://twitter.com/darrenrovell/status/319226838423568384?lang=en.
7. https://tripadvisor.mediaroom.com/2009-07-08-Photos-U-S-Travelers-Peeved-by-Poor-Pool-Practices-and-Bad-Beach-Behavior.
8. https://www.youtube.com/watch?v=toH4GcPQXpc.
9. https://www.sportengland.org/our-work/women/this-girl-can/.
10. https://the-dots.com/projects/this-girl-can-case-study-142741.
11. http://shortyawards.com/7th/all-things-hair-big-hair-meets-big-data.

12. http://www.rohitbhargava.com/2014/10/5-corporate
    -storytelling-lessons-from-beth-comstock.html.
13. https://www.ishmaelscorner.com/warren-buffetts
    -storytelling-transforms-shareholders-letter/.
14. https://www.ishmaelscorner.com/storytelling-in-warren
    -buffet-shareholder-letter/.
15. https://twitter.com/arbys/status/427614008946855936
    ?lang=en.
16. https://twitter.com/Pharrell/status/427733647081209856.

Chapter 4

1. https://www.united.com/web/en-US/content/customerfirst
   .aspx.
2. http://www.brandindex.com/article/united-airlines-hits
   -lowest-consumer-perception-10-years.
3. https://blogs.gartner.com/jake-sorofman/gartner-surveys
   -confirm-customer-experience-new-battlefield/.
4. https://twitter.com/Casper/status/963822897193213957.
5. https://twitter.com/Casper/status/963430562731036672.
6. https://twitter.com/Casper/status/964880568805621763.
7. http://insomnobot3000.com/.
8. http://uk.businessinsider.com/how-the-200-million-startup
   -casper-is-looking-to-upend-advertising-2017-7.
9. http://blog.casper.com/the-sleep-symposium/.
10. http://shortyawards.com/9th/wearecisco-employee
    -engagement-for-talent-bran.
11. http://shortyawards.com/9th/wearecisco-employee
    -engagement-for-talent-bran.
12. http://www/cisco.com/c/en/us/about/careers/html.
13. https://blogs.cisco.com/lifeatcisco/may-the-4th-be-with
    -you.
14. https://blogs.cisco.com/lifeatcisco/may-the-4th-be-with
    -you.
15. https://business.linkedin.com/elevate.
16. http://www.convinceandconvert.com/social-media-case
    -studies/could-buymybarina-be-the-best-used-car-ad-ever/.
17. http://www.campaignbrief.com/2014/08/nrma-insurance
    -buys-barina-you.html.
18. http://www.t-sciences.com/news/humans-process-visual
    -data-better.

19. https://blog.hubspot.com/blog/tabid/6307/bid/33423/19
-reasons-you-should-include-visual-content-in-your-marketing
-data.aspx.
20. http://www.jeffbullas.com/visual-content-marketing
-statistics/.
21. https://www.socialpilot.co/blog/social-media-statistics.
22. https://www.theatlantic.com/health/archive/2014/11/the
-psychological-comforts-of-storytelling/381964/.
23. https://grasshopper.com/resources/case-studies/grass
hopper-rebranding/.
24. https://www.instagram.com/p/BfKaJzQnn-6/?taken-by=tsa.
25. https://www.instagram.com/p/BX1aDCMjJNu/?hl=en&
taken-by=tsa.
26. https://blog.flixel.com/flixel-microsoft-case-study/.
27. https://twitter.com/TheRitas/status/966735460679733248.
28. https://twitter.com/savvybostonian/status/96858969049549
2096.
29. https://twitter.com/TheRitas/status/968615281030500353.
30. https://www.columnfivemedia.com/work-items/infographic
-the-search-for-the-pink-unicorn.
31. https://www.jobvite.com/resource_type/infographic/.
32. https://www.slideshare.net/Experian_US/how-to-save-on
-holiday-travel.
33. http://www.adweek.com/agencies/kfc-wrote-a-romance
-novel-for-mothers-day-and-its-uncomfortably-good/.
34. http://www.jessicagioglio.com/land-rover-tumblr-novel/.
35. https://animoto.com/blog/business/video-marketing-cheat
-sheet-infographic/.
36. https://www.forbes.com/sites/ajagrawal/2017/02/01/lights
-camera-engagement-2017-is-the-year-of-video-marketing/
#6d2c57542315.
37. https://digiday.com/media/silent-world-facebook-video/.
38. http://go.ooyala.com/rs/447-EQK-225/images/Ooyala
-Global-Video-Index-Q2-2016.pdf.
39. https://visitfaroeislands.com/sheepview360/.
40. https://www.adforum.com/creative-work/ad/player
/34547373/google-sheep-view-case-film/visit-faroe-islands.
41. https://www.adforum.com/creative-work/ad/player
/34547373/google-sheep-view-case-film/visit-faroe-islands.
42. http://www.zdnet.com/blog/feeds/smart-usa-does-the
-math-on-twitter-about-pigeon-crap/4921.

43. http://time.com/4745066/adidas-boston-marathon-email/.
44. http://www.adweek.com/creativity/american-apparel-gap-blasted-hurricane-sandy-ad-fails-144905/.
45. http://info.localytics.com/blog/mobile-apps-whats-a-good-retention-rate.
46. http://bigthink.com/design-for-good/the-first-billboard-in-the-world-to-make-drinking-water-out-of-thin-ai.
47. https://blogs.gartner.com/jake-sorofman/gartner-surveys-confirm-customer-experience-new-battlefield/.
48. https://www.econsultancy.com/blog/69269-17-stats-that-show-why-cx-is-so-important.
49. http://fortune.com/2017/01/09/california-woman-sues-chipotle-for-2-2-billion-over-using-her-photograph/.
50. http://mediakix.com/2017/03/instagram-influencer-marketing-industry-size-how-big/#gs.4nVtBWA.
51. http://mediakix.com/2017/05/celebrity-social-media-endorsements-violate-ftc-instagram/#gs.lKZo8vM.
52. https://www.ftc.gov/news-events/press-releases/2016/07/warner-bros-settles-ftc-charges-it-failed-adequately-disclose-it.
53. https://www.ftc.gov/news-events/blogs/business-blog/2017/04/influencers-are-your-materialconnection-disclosures.
54. https://www.cbsnews.com/news/h-m-the-weeknd-coolest-monkey-in-the-jungle-racist-hoodie/.
55. https://www.parents.com/blogs/parents-news-now/2013/08/07/must-read/the-childrens-place-apologizes-for-offensive-girls-t-shirt-2/.
56. https://www.nytimes.com/2018/02/06/business/lady-doritos-indra-nooyi.html.
57. https://www.nytimes.com/2018/02/06/business/lady-doritos-indra-nooyi.html.
58. https://www.fastcompany.com/40528577/lady-doritos-were-not-good-for-the-doritos-brand.
59. http://www.coca-colacompany.com/coca-cola-unbottled/every-day-is-election-day.

Chapter 5

1. https://www.campaignlive.co.uk/article/case-study-oreo-eclipse/1366744#VTGQ0UfjwK4Um7Km.99.
2. https://www.youtube.com/watch?v=3mvr1F9GCLo.

3. http://www.adweek.com/digital/taco-bells-cinco-de-mayo -snapchat-lens-was-viewed-224-million-times-171390/.

4. http://www.adweek.com/agencies/this-creative-agency -made-poster-sized-bacteria-filled-petri-dishes-and-put -them-in-a-mall/.

5. https://www.accenture.com/us-en/insight-hyper-relevance -gcpr.

6. https://www.accenture.com/us-en/insight-hyper-relevance -gcpr.

7. https://www.accenture.com/us-en/insight-hyper-relevance -gcpr.

8. https://www.forbes.com/sites/kashmirhill/2012/02/16/how -target-figured-out-a-teen-girl-was-pregnant-before-her -father-did/.

9. https://www.aspect.com/globalassets/aspect-consumer -experience-index-state-of-cx.pdf.

10. https://www.aspect.com/globalassets/aspect-consumer -experience-index-state-of-cx.pdf.

11. https://www.aspect.com/globalassets/aspect-consumer -experience-index-state-of-cx.pdf.

12. https://www.cebglobal.com/blogs/putting-a-human-face-on -customer-effort/.

13. https://www.aspect.com/globalassets/aspect-consumer -experience-index-state-of-cx.pdf.

14. https://www.aspect.com/globalassets/aspect-consumer -experience-index-state-of-cx.pdf.

15. http://www.adweek.com/digital/social-media-accounts/.

16. https://www.statista.com/statistics/273288/advertising -spending-worldwide/.

17. https://www.statista.com/statistics/273288/advertising -spending-worldwide/.

18. https://research.hubspot.com/why-people-block-ads-and -what-it-means-for-marketers-and-advertisers.

19. https://research.hubspot.com/native-advertising-rises-as -consumers-opt-out.

20. https://research.hubspot.com/why-people-block-ads-and -what-it-means-for-marketers-and-advertisers.

21. https://www.facebook.com/business/news/value-of -storytelling-on-facebook.

22. https://www.facebook.com/business/news/value-of -storytelling-on-facebook.

23. https://www.facebook.com/business/news/value-of-storytelling-on-facebook.
24. https://blog.hubspot.com/marketing/blogging-frequency-benchmarks.
25. https://blog.hubspot.com/marketing/blogging-frequency-benchmarks.
26. https://blog.hubspot.com/.
27. https://blog.hubspot.com/marketing/blog-lead-generation-analysis.
28. https://research.hubspot.com/compounding-blog-posts-what-they-are-and-why-they-matter.
29. http://www.wholefoodsmarket.com/blog/whole-story.
30. http://blog.homedepot.com/.
31. http://blog.homedepot.com/become-a-contributor/.
32. https://www.weightwatchers.com/us/connect.
33. http://www.doyouvespa.com/en/manifesto/.
34. http://www.coca-colacompany.com/coca-cola-unbottled/every-day-is-election-day.
35. http://www.coca-colacompany.com/coca-cola-unbottled/every-day-is-election-day.
36. https://en.wikipedia.org/wiki/History_of_podcasting.
37. https://www.podcastinsights.com/podcast-statistics/.
38. http://www.edisonresearch.com/wp-content/uploads/2018/03/Infinite-Dial-2018.pdf.
39. https://www.podcastinsights.com/podcast-statistics/.
40. http://shortyawards.com/10th/hackable-podcast.
41. http://shortyawards.com/10th/hackable-podcast.
42. http://shortyawards.com/10th/hackable-podcast.
43. https://www.fastcompany.com/3068896/ebay-set-to-launch-second-season-of-branded-podcast-open-for-business.
44. http://www.adweek.com/brand-marketing/inside-mcdonalds-new-serial-style-podcast-telling-its-side-of-the-szechuan-sauce-story/.
45. http://www.edisonresearch.com/wp-content/uploads/2018/03/Infinite-Dial-2018.pdf.
46. https://www.fastcompany.com/40533210/branded-podcasts-are-the-ads-people-actually-want-to-listen-to.
47. https://www.marketwatch.com/story/the-booming-smart-speaker-market-and-the-services-it-will-help-2018-01-18.

48. https://techcrunch.com/2017/11/08/voice-enabled-smart
-speakers-to-reach-55-of-u-s-households-by-2022-says
-report/.
49. https://www.marketwatch.com/story/the-booming-smart
-speaker-market-and-the-services-it-will-help-2018-01-18.
50. https://www.amazon.com/BMW-Technology-Group
-Connected/dp/B01LWLCMGF.
51. https://www.amazon.com/P-G-Productions-Tide
-Remover/dp/B01M9B7ZTB.
52. https://www.amazon.com/Johnnie-Walker/dp/B01LZSIYV5
/ref=sr_1_1?s=digital-skills&ie=UTF8&qid=1520794090&sr
=1-1&keywords=johnnie+walker.
53. https://www.amazon.com/Warner-Bros-The-Wayne
-Investigation/dp/B01C9AX5VY/ref=sr_1_1?s=digital-skills&i
e=UTF8&qid=1520790263&sr=1-1&keywords=warner+bros.

Chapter 6

1. https://sproutsocial.com/insights/data/q2-2016/.
2. https://econsultancy.com/blog/7403-how-many-bad
-reviews-does-it-take-to-deter-shoppers#i.nzb6rp178cdwxz.
3. https://www.tripadvisor.com/TripAdvisorInsights/n2428
/how-add-management-responses-tripadvisor-traveler
-reviews.
4. http://www.retailing.org/knowledge_center/sites/default
/files/The_Retail_Consumer_Report.pdf.
5. https://www.entrepreneur.com/article/246053.
6. https://econsultancy.com/blog/65752-klm-we-make-25m
-per-year-from-social-media/.
7. http://www.paullyoung.com/2013/12/09/citibike-love/.
8. https://www.campaignlive.co.uk/article/mcdonalds-honest
-approach-fast-food/1343221#jBk82zB1RsYKlqfP.99.

INDEX

Acknowledging complaints, 236
Action:
  aligned with purpose, 258
  on customer complaints, 237–238
Actionable Intelligence Law,
  106–114
AdAge, 25
Adding value, 116–117
Adidas, 181
Ads, 214–217
Advocacy, 51–53, 142–145
Agile marketing, 178
Airbnb, 49–51, 137
AKQA, 34
Alaska Airlines, 248–249
All Things Hair, 117
#AllTreesAreBeautiful, 54–56
Amazon Wines, 82
Ambassador programs, 81–82, 104
American Apparel, 25, 181–182
Andreassen, Durita Dahl, 173
Annex, 62–63
Annual reports, 126, 128
Apologies, 55, 237, 248
Applbaum, Lee, 107–108
Apple, 215
Apple Podcasts, 224
Arby's, 129
Authenticity, 16
  as Achilles' heel, 40
  in apologies, 237
  defining, 40
  of stories, 94
  in This Girl Can campaign, 113
  in tone of voice, 138–139
  in utilitarian marketing, 190
Authenticity Law, 38–45
Authenticity Playbook, 40–43,
  51–53, 199

Balenciaga, 160
Banish the Buzzwords, 158, 159
Behavior, consistency of, 133–134
Behind-the-scenes activities,
  114–115
Berkshire Hathaway, 126

Beyond-the-Obvious Law, 114–120
Bezos, Jeff, 106
Bic, 196
Birchbox, 250
Blogs, 217–219
BMW Connected, 229
Boff, Linda, 52–53
Borrow My Doggy, 12–13
Boyd, William, 168
Brand, defined, 3
Brand DNA, 65, 68
Brand guidelines, 40–41
Brand identity, 3
Brand Protection Law, 193–199
Brand storytelling, 1–9
  definitions of, 3, 4
  holistic approach to, 8–9
  macro stories, 4–5
  micro stories, 5–6
  by REI, 2, 6–8
  The Storyteller Journey, 9
  to support mission, 6
Branding, 3
Branson, Richard, 21
Brown, Ashley, 222
Buffer, 20
Buffett, Warren, 126, 128
Burck, Robert John, 76
Burritt, Linsey, 48
#BuyMyBarina, 146–148

Cadbury, 5
Caldwell, Leah, 191
Calgary Zoo, 126
Cancer Council Australia, 147
Career Builder, 215
Caring, 129
Carl's Jr., 68–71
Carnegie, Dale, 20
Cartoons, 156–159
Casper, 139–142
Casper the Blog, 140
Celebrating non-obvious
  occasions, 115–116
"Championing Change in the Age
  of Social Media," 49, 51

Chanel, 160
Change, 170–171, 247
Channel Laws, 205–231
  Channel Mix Law, 211–231
  Personalization Law, 207–210
Channel Mix Law, 211–231
  strategy considerations, 211–213
  types of channels, 213–231
Character:
  of NKD Wines, 77
  in tone of voice, 138
Charmin, 94, 187
Chief experience officer, 90
The Children's Place, 196
Chipotle Mexican Grill, 191
Cinco de Mayo Snapchat
    Sponsored Lens, 207
Cinemagraphs, 158, 160
Cisco, 121–122, 142–145, 176, 251
Citi Bike, 240–241, 244
CKE Restaurants, 68
Coca-Cola, 15, 27, 202–203, 222–223
The Coca-Cola Journey, 222–223
Codes of Culture, 62, 66
Cole Haan, 194
Collaboration Law, 90–91
Colors, 26–28, 79
Comedy (see Humor)
Communities, 233–234
  customer, 219–221
  engaging with (see Laws of
      Engagement)
Complaints, handling, 236–238
Compounding posts, 218
Comstock, Beth, 121
Concierge service, 250
Conflict Law, 45–57
  aligning advocacy and
      Authenticity Playbook, 51–53
  and silence vs. speaking
      out, 49–51
  and standing up for
      yourself, 54–57
Connect, 219
Consistency:
  across touchpoints, 138
  for authenticity, 45
  of behavior, 133–134
  of customer experience, 135–136
  dimensions of, 132–133
  of engagement, 134–135
  of message, 134

in podcasting, 228
of promise, 134
of publishing, 135
Consistency Law, 132–136
Consumers:
  conversations/stories of, 65–66
  as heroes of stories, 96
Content:
  change in, 170–171
  creating, 135
  educational, 224
  80/20 rule for, 235
  marrying context with, 153–155
  Ownership Law for, 191–193
  quality of, 171–174
  visual vs. text-based, 170
Context, marrying content with,
    153–155
"Continuous Candidate
    Engagement—Why You Need
    CCE," 165
Crafting your story (see Story-
    Making Laws; Storytelling
    framework)
Crave Culture, 68–71
Creative bets, 66
Creative journey, sharing, 119
#CreditChat, 166–167
Cultural Point of View (POV), 66,
    68, 71
Culture:
  codes of, 62, 66, 68, 71
  company, 17–19, 63
  and customer experience, 67–68
  emerging, 62–63
  of NKD Wines, 87
  of sharing stories, 144–145
  showcasing, 251
  "story culture," 121
  that rewards employee
      advocacy, 143
Customer communities, 219–221
Customer experience, 258
  consistency of, 135–136
  and culture, 67–68
  online stories of, 104
  personality in, 33–34
  personalized, 209
  stories in, 90
  with utilitarian marketing,
      189–190
  values aligned with, 22

Customer experience management (CXM), 90, 178–179
Customer insights, 111–114
Customer preferences, in visuals, 168–169
Customer-centric stories, 257
Customers' customers, looking at needs of, 119–120

#DailyTwist, 183
Dalai Lama XIV, 254
Dale, Kate, 113
Danzie, Jay, 33
Dave (epic strut), 29–30
Defining moments, 73
Dell, 28
Differentiation Law, 29–38
Differentiator(s):
    in attracting target audience, 33–35
    for customer communities, 221
    customer experience as, 136
    in Strategic Blueprint, 72
    working your, 30–32
Digimind, 197
Digital magazines, 221–224
Digital media, as 24/7 focus group, 106–108
The Dirtbag Diaries, 1–2
Disclosures, 193–195
Discovery Laws, 93–129
    Actionable Intelligence Law, 106–114
    Beyond-the-Obvious Law, 114–120
    Hero Law, 95–106
    Law of Opportunity, 124–129
    Storyteller Law, 120–123
Disruptors, 254
Diversification Law, 156–171
    cartoons, 156–159
    cinemagraphs, 158, 160
    GIFs, 160–162
    infographics, 165–166
    key considerations, 168–171
    memes, 163–164
    presentations, 166–167
    white papers and e-Books, 167–169
Do You Vespa?, 219–221
"Do Your Part[ner]," 96, 100–104
Dollar Shave Club, 14–16

Doritos, 196–199
Dreams, 1–2
Dresselhaus, Millie, 52, 53
Dubin, Michael, 14–15
Dunkin' Donuts, 28–29, 109–110, 115–116, 139

"Eat Like a Lady," 199
eBay, 225–226
e-Books, 167–169
Educating, 118–119, 224
The Electric Factory Group, 207–208
Emirates Airline, 125
Emojiscience.com, 120
Employees:
    as advocates, 142–145
    feedback from, 20–21, 102
    telling stories of, 117–118
Engadget.com, 107
Engagement:
    consistency of, 134–135
    on daily basis, 179
    Laws of (*see* Laws of Engagement)
    through cartoons, 156–157
#EpicStrut, 30, 33
Evans, M'Lynn, 1–2
Evans, Paul, 1–2
Execution, 255
Experian, 166–167

The Face-to-Face Book (Ed Keller and Bray Fay), 243
Farrar, Corina, 87
"Fast IT and the Slow Waiter," 123
Fay, Bray, 243
Federal Trade Commission (FTC), 193–195
Finding your story (*see* Discovery Laws)
Fiore, Victoria, 97–100, 102
Fishburne, Tom (Marketoonist), 157–159
Ford, 15
404 pages, 125
"The Full Monty," 126, 127
Fun, 87, 121–123 (*See also* Humor)

Gap, 24–26
Gascoigne, Joel, 20
Ge-girls.com, 120

General Electric (GE), 28, 51–53, 119–120, 139, 160, 224
GIFs, 160–162
Girl Scouts, 28
Gizmodo, 226
Global Brand Simplicity Index, 137
Goals, understanding (*see* Strategy Laws)
Godin, Seth, 135
Goidel, Melissa, 215
Google, 173–174
GotVMail, 162
Grace Hopper Celebration of Women Conference, 143
Grand Hyatt, 244–246
Grasshopper, 162–163
"G-Rated Quickies," 101
Gregory, Gregg, 105–106
Grover, Crystal, 48

Hackable, 225
Hall, Kathleen, 43
Halo effect, 119, 144–145, 189–190
Hansen, Marka, 25–26
Hardee's, 68, 71
Havas, 62–72
HEART culture code (HubSpot), 23–24
Heart marketing, 258
Hero Law, 95–106
  Kelleher's leadership, 104–106
  Plum Organics stories, 96–104
Heroes:
  in Borrow My Doggy story, 13
  customers as, 257
  of macro and micro stories, 95
History of company, 72, 121
H&M, 195–196
Holden Barina, 145–148
Holidays, nonstandard, 115–116
Home Depot, 218–219
Honda, 160
Honey Maid, 45–48
Hove, Clayton, 175
"How to Save on Holiday Travel," 167
How to Win Friends and Influence People (Dale Carnegie), 20
How-to videos, 116–117
Hsieh, Tony, 18, 19
HubSpot, 22–24, 117, 217–218
Huffington, Arianna, 141

Humanizing your brand:
  Law of, 248–251
  through self-deprecating humor, 176
  with tone of your message, 138–142 (*See also* Language Law)
  and visual brand identity, 26
Humor, 43–44
  cartoons, 156–159
  memes, 163–164
  Washer's use of, 121–123
  (*See also* Fun)
Humor Law, 174–177

IBM, 28
Ideas, developing, 63–66
Identity:
  of NKD Wines, 77, 78
  in Strategic Blueprint, 72
  visual, 151–153
  Visual Identity Law, 24–29
  (*See also* Protagonist Laws)
IKEA Singapore, 163–164
Influencers:
  building relationships with, 102
  events for, 104
  and FTC guidelines, 193–195
Infobesity, 150, 151, 177, 186
Infographics, 165–166
Innovators, partnering with, 145–148
Insomnobot-3000, 141
Inspiration, 118–119, 254
Instagram influencer marketing, 193
Intel, 28, 114–115, 192
Interactions, as opportunities, 108–110
Interactive voice response (IVR), 210

Jobvite, 165
Johnnie Walker, 230
Johns, David, 145–148

Kaplan, Lindsay, 141
Kelleher, Herb, 104–106
Keller, Ed, 243
Kenneth Cole, 181
KFC, 34–35, 167–168
KLM, 238–239
K9 Ballistics, 180

Knowing who you are (*see* Identity; Protagonist Laws)
Kraft Foods, 4–5

Land Rover, 168
Language Law, 138–148
    being voice customers want to hear, 139–142
    partnering with innovators, 145–148
    tapping employee advocates, 142–145
Late Night Snap Hacks, 141
"The Law of Employee Attraction," 165
Law of Humanizing Your Brand, 248–251
Law of Opportunity, 124–129
Laws of Engagement, 233–251
    Law of Humanizing Your Brand, 248–251
    Response Law, 234–240
    Surprise and Delight Law, 240–248
Leap Day, 19
Lego, 125
Les Schwab Amphitheater, 80
Life After podcast, 224
Life at Cisco blog, 142, 143
Lime-A-Rita, 161–162
LinkedIn, 157–159
Listening, 129, 234
Local partnerships, 85
The Logo Company, 27
Logos, 4, 24–27, 79
Lord & Taylor, 194
Lyft, 137

Macro stories, 4–5, 90, 95
Maersk, 94–95
Magners Cider, 160
Makers Movement, 117
Making your own laws, 253–255
Marketoonist, 157–159
#Maythe4th, 143–144
McAfee, 225
McDonald, Robert, 147
McDonald's, 226, 250
Media events, 104
"Meet the Ritas," 161–162
Memes, 163–164
Mentality shifts, 257–259

Mercedes, 243–244
Message:
    consistency of, 134
    tone of, 138–142
The Message podcast, 224
Micro stories, 5–6, 90, 95
Microsoft, 160
Mission:
    aligning Authenticity Playbook with, 41–42
    defining, 13
    evolution of, 22–24
    (*See also specific companies*)
Mistakes:
    apologizing for, 248
    learning/adapting from, 108
Moneysupermarket.com, 30–33
Monty, Scott, 126, 127
Mycoskie, Black, 16–17

Naked Cowboy Wines, 76
Naked Winery, 76, 77, 87, 90
NASA, 179, 184
NASDAQ, 29, 143
Nationwide, 188
Netflix, 27
The New Yorker, 58
Nike, 34
NKD Wines, 76–90
Nooyi, Indra, 196–197
NRMA Insurance, 147–148

Obama, Barack, 161
Offensive campaigns, 195–199
Oh! Orgasmic Wine Co., 76
Olson, Peggy, 161
"The One for One® Company," 17
One Million Moms, 47
The Onion, 226
Open for Business podcast, 225–226
Opportunities:
    customer touchpoints and interactions as, 108–110
    real-time, 129
    for storytelling, 124–125 (*See also* Law of Opportunity)
Optimization Law, 199–203
#OptOutside, 2, 6–7
Oreo, 183, 205–206
#OreoEclipse, 206
Organic Valley, 39–40
Osifchin, Gary, 46, 58

"Our Blades Are F***ing Great," 15
"Our Food. Your Questions.," 250
Outdoor Vino, 76
Ownership Law, 191–193

Parenting Survival Kits, 104
#ParentingUnfiltered, 97–99
Parker, Anna, 62, 67
Patagonia, 49
Paul's Boots, 2
#PaulWalksOn, 2
People (in 6Ps Framework), 182
Personal brands, differentiation
    of, 36–38
Personality:
  in attracting target
    audience, 33–35
  defining, 13
  as differentiator, 31–32
  of NKD Wines, 79–80
  showcasing, 28
  in tone of voice, 138
  values shaping, 16
Personalization Law, 207–210
Phone cameras, 171
Piaggio, 219–221
Planning (in 6Ps Framework),
    183–184
Playbook (in 6Ps Framework),
    184–185
Plum Organics, 96–104
Podcasts, 224–228
Possibilities, 90
The Power of Visual Storytelling
    (Ekaterina Walter and Jessica
    Gioglio), 8–9, 27, 155–156
Practice (in 6Ps Framework), 184
Prange, Stephanie, 79–81
Preparation (in 6Ps
    Framework), 183
Presentations, 166–167
Priming-and-reminding
    storytelling, 216–217
Process (in 6Ps Framework), 182
Products, misconception
    about, 94–95
Promise(s):
  consistency of, 134
  delivering on, 258
Protagonist Laws, 11–57
  Authenticity Law, 38–45
  Conflict Law, 45–57

Differentiation Law, 29–38
  Purpose Law, 14–24
  Visual Identity Law, 24–29
Publishing, consistency of, 135
Purpose Law, 14–24
  being true to brand values, 16–17
  culture you want to
    nurture, 17–19
  defining and communicating
    values, 19–24
  reason for your brand's
    existence, 14–16

Quality Law, 171–174

RadioShack, 107–108
"Real Morning Report," 39–40
#RealGravity, 179
Reality, staying grounded in, 21
Real-time marketing, 177–186
Real-time opportunities, 129
Recreational Equipment, Inc. (REI),
    1–2, 6–8
Reese's, 54–56
Refinery29, 215
Relevance, 51, 177, 254
Reps, identified by name, 248–249
Reputation, 17–18
Residence Inn, 244, 246–247
Response Law, 234–240
Responsiveness, 179–181
Rhett and Link, 199
Ridiculous Media, 121
Risk taking, 129, 255
#RitaSays, 161–162
Robbins, Chuck, 144
Rosenlund, Rikke, 11–13
Rovell, Darren, 110
Royal Dutch Airlines KLM,
    238–239

Samsung, 188–189
The Sauce podcast, 225
Schneider Electric, 158
"The Search for the Pink
    Unicorn," 165
Seasonal products, 82–85
Seek & Swoon, 36–38
Sequential storytelling, 215
Shah, Dharmesh, 23
Shareholder letters, 126, 128
Sheep View 360, 172–174

Shelf Help Guru, 163–164
Shutterstock, 125
Siegel+Gale, 137
Silence, speaking out vs., 49–51
Silos, 90
Simon, Carly, 96
Simplicity Law, 136–138
Sinek, Simon, 14
SitorSquat Restroom Finder, 187
6Ps Framework, 182–186
Size, differentiation and, 36–38
Sleep Symposium, 141–142
Smart Car, 174–175
Smart speakers, 229–230
Smith-Huys, Jala, 36–38
Sobel, Katie, 97, 102
Social capital, depositing
    into, 42–45
Social data, 65–66
Social media:
    as 24/7 focus group, 106–108
    command center for, 184–185
    companies' use of (see individual
        companies)
    number of channels per user, 211
        (See also Channel Mix Law)
    responding to messages/
        comments on, 134–136,
        234–240
Soma Intimates, 241–243
Sony, 194
Southwest Airlines, 15, 104–106
Speaking out, silence vs., 49–51
"A Special Valentine's Day Gift . . .
    from Cisco!," 121–122
Sport England, 112–114
Sprout Social, 49, 51
Standing up for yourself, 54–57
Starbucks, 28
Story(-ies):
    elements in, 73
    episodic, 224
    heroes of, 95–106
    leveraging insights to change,
        112–114
    macro, 4–5, 90, 95
    memory of facts vs., 151
    micro, 5–6, 90, 95–96
    misconceptions about, 94
    in Strategic Blueprint, 72 (See also
        Storytelling framework)
"Story culture," 121

Story-Making Laws, 131–203
    Brand Protection Law, 193–199
    Consistency Law, 132–136
    Diversification Law, 156–171
    Humor Law, 174–177
    Language Law, 138–148
    Optimization Law, 199–203
    Ownership Law, 191–193
    Quality Law, 171–174
    Simplicity Law, 136–138
    Urgency Law, 177–186
    Utility Law, 186–191
    Visual Storytelling Law, 148–156
The Storyteller Journey, 9
Storyteller Law, 120–123
Storytelling framework:
    elements of, 74–75
    of Havas, 63–67, 70–71
    macro and micro stories in, 90
    in Strategic Blueprint Law, 74–90
Strategic Blueprint Law, 60–90
    approach in, 62–74
    defining strategy in, 60–62
    storytelling framework in, 74–90
Strategy:
    defining, 60–62
    incorporating humor in, 122–123
    key elements of, 60–61
Strategy Laws, 59–91
    Collaboration Law, 90–91
    Strategic Blueprint Law, 60–90
Strayed, Cheryl, 7–8
Stuart Weitzman, 160
The Sun, 205–206
Surprise and Delight Law, 240–248
Swedish Childhood Cancer
    Foundation, 149

Taco Bell, 207
Taking a stand, 49–57
Target, 27, 208–209
Target audience:
    attracting, 33–35
    stories focused on, 94
#TeamParent, 104
Technologizer.com, 107
TempurPedic, 180
Tender Wings of Desire (KFC), 35,
    167–168
Tesco, 43–44
Thank You pages, 125–127
This Girl Can, 113–114

"This Is Wholesome," 45–48
Three As, for complaints, 236–238
Thunderclap, 47
Tide, 185
Tide Stain Remover, 229, 231
Tilden, Brad, 249
"The Toilet Index," 210
TOMS, 16–17, 49
TOMS Bags, 17
TOMS Roasting Co., 17
Tone:
  of NKD Wines, 77
  of voice, 138–142 (See also
    Language Law)
Top assets, working your, 30–32
Torrey, Tatia, 62, 66–68
Touchpoints:
  consistency across, 138
  marketing ideas for, 124–125
  as opportunities, 108–110
Transparency, 249–250
TripAdvisor, 111–112
Trump, Donald, 49
TSA, 153–155
Tung, Eric, 244–247

Uber, 137
Unbottled blog, 202–203, 223
Understanding your goals (see
  Strategy Laws)
Unilever, 16, 117
United Airlines, 106, 133–134
University of Engineering and
  Technology of Peru, 188
Urgency Law, 177–186
User-generated content (UGC), 192
Utility Law, 186–191

Value:
  adding, 116–117
  through real-time stories/
    content/responses, 179
Value proposition, as
  differentiator, 31–32
Values:
  aligning Authenticity Playbook
    with, 41–42
  being true to, 16–17
  communicating, 19–24
  in culture, 18–19
  defining, 13, 19–24
  evolution of, 22–24

standing up for, 49–57
  in Strategic Blueprint, 72
  in tone of voice, 138
Van Halen, 247–248
The Vanishing Game, 168
Venmo, 137
Vibe, in differentiation, 33–35
Virgin Group, 21
Visit Faroe Islands, 172–174
Visual identity, 151–153
Visual Identity Law, 24–29
Visual mix, 156, 169–170 (See also
  Diversification Law)
Visual Storytelling Law, 148–156
Visuals:
  evaluating channels for, 155
  identity reflected in, 151–153
  memory of, 151
  selecting, 168–171
  Visual Identity Law, 24–29
Voice:
  in employee social media
    messages, 144
  in Strategic Blueprint, 72
  tone of, 138–142
  values shaping, 16
Voice assistants, 228–231
Voxbone, 35

Walt Disney, 15
Warner Bros., 194, 230
Washer, Tim, 121–123, 175–176
The Wayne Investigation, 230
#WeAccept, 49–51
#WeAreCisco, 142–143, 251
Weight Watchers, 219
Wendy's, 239–240
White papers, 167–169
Whole Foods, 28, 218
Widrich, Leo, 20
Wild (movie), 7–8
Williams, Pharrell, 129
Williamson, Cory Cae, 82–83, 87
Wired.com, 107
Woolly Magazine, 140

Xbox, 194

Young, Paull, 240–241, 244
"Your Year with Nike+," 34

Zappos, 18–19, 117–118, 241

ABOUT THE AUTHORS

Ekaterina **Walter** is a globally recognized business and marketing innovator, international speaker, and author of the *Wall Street Journal* bestseller *Think Like Zuck* and coauthor of *The Power of Visual Storytelling*. After pioneering social media and digital strategies for Fortune 500 brands such as Intel and Accenture, she cofounded a start-up that was acquired by Sprinklr, a customer experience management platform, where she served as Global Evangelist. She now helps global organizations build customer-centric digital transformation strategies.

Ekaterina's thought leadership has been featured on CNBC, ABC, NBC, FOX News, Forbes, Fast Company, TechCrunch, CNN, WSJ, Inc., and Huffington Post, among others. She's been consistently recognized by the industry and her peers for her innovative thinking: she was number three on Forbes's World's Top 40 Social Marketing Talent, and *Fortune* magazine included her on the list of the most impactful business people on social media, alongside Bill Gates, Oprah Winfrey, Arianna Huffington, Warren Buffet, and others.

When Ekaterina is not writing about digital and business innovation, she and her nine-year-old daughter coauthor children's books. The first of a planned series, *Amber and Sapphire: The Magic Spell*, was published in 2017.

Walter holds a master's degree in international management from Thunderbird School of Global Management at Arizona State University. You can chat with her on Twitter @Ekaterina or find out more about her on *EkaterinaWalter.com*.

Jessica Gioglio is a recognized digital and social business strategist and the coauthor of *The Power of Visual Storytelling*. She has spent over a decade leading transformative marketing, public relations, and social media programs for best-in-class companies including Dunkin' Donuts, Trip Advisor, State Street, Comcast, and Sprinklr.

From advising top companies on social media and digital business transformation, to leading an award-winning public relations and social media program for Dunkin' Donuts, or providing disruptive communications programs for TripAdvisor, Jessica thrives on delivering customer-centric innovation and growth acceleration.

A recognized thought leader and sought-after speaker, Jessica was named one of the top marketing leaders to follow by LinkedIn, HubSpot, TopRank Online Marketing, and the United Kingdom's We Are The City. Jessica's thought leadership and industry commentary have been featured on CNBC, USA Today, PR Week, ComputerWorld, Chief Marketer, and more.

Jessica holds a bachelor of science degree in marketing from Bentley University, with a minor in public relations. In her spare time, Jessica explores the world and writes about her adventures on her lifestyle blog, *TheSavvyBostonian.com*. You can also find her on Twitter @savvybostonian and on her website, *JessicaGioglio.com*.